Der Potsdamer Platz

Urban architecture
for a new Berlin

Urbane Architektur
für das neue Berlin

Herausgegeben von
Edited by
Yamin von Rauch
Jochen Visscher

Fotografien von
Photographs by
Alexander Schippel

Mit Beiträgen von
With articles by
Roland Enke
Werner Sewing
Hans Wilderotter

jovis

Gestaltung/Design
Christoph Holzki, Satzinform, Berlin

Umschlagfoto/Cover photography
Alexander Schippel

Der Fotograf dankt
Labor Pixel Grain
Fachlabor für Photographie
für die freundliche Zusammenarbeit

Satz und Lithographie/Typesetting and lithography
Satzinform, Berlin

Druck und Bindung/Printing and binding
Offizin Andersen Nexö Leipzig, Zwenkau

Übersetzung ins Englische/English translation
Ian Cowley: Vorwort/preface, Essay/essay
H. Wilderotter; Michael Dills: Essays/essays R. Enke,
W. Sewing

ISBN 3-931321-95-9

Inhalt

Contents

Der Potsdamer Platz

Berlins bekanntester Platz ist er seit langem schon. Erklären kann man seine Berühmtheit, ja seinen Mythos, eigentlich nicht, denn nie war er in seiner Vergangenheit ein idealtypischer Platz, wohlproportioniert und geordnet, dekoriert mit Gartenanlagen und Brunnen, von reizvollen Gebäuden umgeben. Er war allenfalls eine – wenn auch wichtige – Straßenkreuzung im Zentrum der deutschen Hauptstadt. Damals wurde er gerühmt von zahlreichen Literaten und weniger bekannten Schreibern, sein Name stand für Geschäftigkeit und Verkehr, für Amüsement und Nachtleben, kurzum, für alle Attribute einer richtigen Metropole. Nicht müde wurde man schon seinerzeit, dessen Großstadteigenschaften mit Superlativen zu preisen: 34 Straßenbahnlinien und Europas verkehrsreichste Autokreuzung, größter U- und S-Bahn-Knotenpunkt; und dann gab es da noch diese berühmte erste Ampelanlage, die im Jahr 1924 – verkehrstechnisch bereits veraltet – einfach auf die Mitte der Kreuzung gesetzt wurde und damit zumindest andeutete, daß da etwas um etwas kreiste. Eine Kopie dieses Verkehrsturms steht seit den späten 90er Jahren unweit der alten Stelle. Bedeutungslos.

In der Phase zwischen Kriegsende und Wiedervereinigung war an diesem innerstädtischen Ort, der nun genau auf der Demarkationslinie dreier Besatzungszonen lag, infolge von Kriegs- und Nachkriegszerstörungen eine riesige Brachfläche entstanden, die immer noch kein Platz war, sondern nun viel Platz für innerstädtische Kaninchen und die Grenztruppen der DDR bot; besichtigt, besucht und fotografiert auch in dieser Zeit – zumindest auf Westseite der Berliner Mauer. Omnibusweise wurden Touristen an diesem tristen Ort abgeladen, der hier feinste Gelegenheit bot, den kommunistischen Osten zu besichtigen – und natürlich die Kaninchen. Er wurde besungen, beschrieben und beklagt, nun war der Potsdamer Platz der traurigste und elendste Ort der Welt, Symbol für die deutsche Teilung und den Kalten Krieg. Und die Berliner hatten ein neues Wahrzeichen.

Potsdamer Platz

It is the most well known square in Berlin, and has been for quite some time. However, its fame, its legendary status even, is something which can't really be explained. This is because it never fitted the ideal typology of a square in the past: well proportioned and ordered, decorated with gardens and fountains, surrounded by charming buildings. It was, at best, a road junction in the centre of the German capital city, albeit an important one. In those days, it was praised by numerous literary figures, and less-well-known writers. Its name stood for bustling activity and traffic, for amusement and night life, in short, for all the attributes of a proper metropolis. Even then, people didn't tire of praising its metropolitan characteristics with superlatives: 34 tram lines, Europe's busiest road junction, and the biggest interchange of underground and suburban trains. Then there was that famous first set of traffic lights which was simply placed in the middle of the junction in 1924, even though it was already obsolete in traffic engineering terms. In doing so, it did at least indicate that something was circling around something there. A copy of this traffic tower has stood close to the old site since the end of the nineties. It is now devoid of all meaning.

In the phase between the end of the Second World War and German reunification, Potsdamer Platz was precisely at the point where the demarcation lines between three occupation sectors met. A huge wasteland arose at this city centre location as a result of destruction, both during and after the war. It was still not a square, but instead now offered a great deal of space for downtown rabbits and the East German border guards. In this phase, too, it was inspected, visited and photographed – on the western side of the Berlin Wall, at least. Tourists were dumped at this dreary place by the bus load. It was a site offering the finest opportunity for viewing the communist East – and, of course, the rabbits. Potsdamer Platz was sung about, de-

Nach 1989 ist immer noch kein Platz aus ihm geworden. An historischem Ort befindet sich heute ein städtebaulicher Raum in beachtlicher Größe von etwa 480.000 m², mit Straßen, Gassen und einem Marlene-Dietrich-Platz, mit Hotels und Cafés, kurzum, einer fast kompletten städtischen Infrastruktur. Schon zu Baustellenzeiten wurde er wiederum gewürdigt und gepriesen. Nun war der Potsdamer Platz plötzlich zur größten Baustelle Europas (oder auch der Welt) geworden. Man erfand den Begriff des Baustellentourismus und tatsächlich stapften Millionen von Besuchern von der roten Info Box durch Matsch und Dreck zu Baulöchern und bestaunten tanzende Kräne. Erklären konnte man das eigentlich nicht.

Auch nach Fertigstellung zahlreicher Gebäude ist er einer der touristischen Magneten Berlins geblieben, der nichts von seiner großen Anziehungskraft verloren zu haben scheint. Er konnte – obwohl doch geschichtslos – ohne Mühen anknüpfen an den eigenen Mythos.

Bei allen äußeren Veränderungen bleibt er standhaft ein Symbol für die Modernität Berlins; mit Ausnahme der Zeit der deutschen Teilung gilt das für die 20er Jahre ebenso wie für die Gegenwart. Dieser Ort weckt keine Erinnerungen. Die »geretteten« Baudenkmale ändern daran nichts. Auch ein Berliner – so Werner Sewing – fühlt sich hier als Tourist, weil er nichts erkennt, nichts erinnert und niemanden kennt. Er ist ein Fremder in der eigenen Stadt; was nichts bedeuten muß, weil ein Berliner – vor allem nach 1989 – mit diesem Gefühl doch allzu gut vertraut ist. Insofern ist der Platz heute sogar ein Ort Neuberliner Identität, also ebenso für den sozialisierten Ost- wie Westberliner, doch insbesondere für den viel unbefangeneren, zugezogenen Berliner, der hier – vielleicht auch aus Mangel an Stadtkenntnis – wirklich weltstädtisches Leben auf kleinstem Raum findet. Ein bißchen von allem und jedem – verwechselbar.

Der Bau des Potsdamer Platzes war ein Experiment. Wo sonst gab es innerhalb einer gewachsenen europäischen Hauptstadt solche Möglichkeiten, ein innerstädtisches Areal voll-

scribed and lamented. Now, though, it was the saddest and most miserable place in the world, a symbol for the division of Germany and the Cold War. Furthermore, the Berliners now had a new symbol.

Since 1989, it still hasn't developed into a square. At the historical site today there is an urban development area of considerable size of around 480,000 square metres, with roads, alleyways, a Marlene-Dietrich-Platz, hotels and cafés. It is, in short, a near-complete urban infrastructure. During the building site era, it was once more appreciated and acclaimed. Now, suddenly, Potsdamer Platz had become the largest building site in Europe (or even the world). The term building site tourism was invented. Millions of visitors really did trudge from the red Info Box through mud and dirt to the construction holes and marvelled at dancing cranes. It couldn't really be explained.

After numerous buildings have been completed, it has remained one of Berlin's tourist magnets. It seems to have lost nothing of its great attraction. It has no history, but it could still easily link up with its own legend. Even with all the external changes, it has remained steadfastly a symbol for the modernity of Berlin. That was true for the nineteen twenties just as much as for today. (The only exception was the period of German division.) This location brings back no memories. The »saved« historical monuments change nothing of that. Werner Sewing claims that Berliners feel like tourists here too because they cannot recognize anything, remember nothing, and know no-one. They are strangers in their own city. That doesn't necessarily mean much, however, after all, the Berliners know this feeling all-too-well, especially since 1989. In this respect, the square today is even a place of new Berlin identity. That is valid for Berliners socialized in the East and West, but especially for the much more impartial Berliners who have moved to the city. At Potsdamer Platz they really do find cosmopolitan life in a small area, even if it may partly be due to a

ständig neu zu planen. Gewichtige Investoren und berühmte Architekten, die die Neugestaltung übernahmen, sollten Qualität garantieren. Das Ergebnis wirft Fragen auf: gelungene Architektur oder vertane Chance, Wagnis oder Mittelmaß, Größenwahn oder vielleicht doch die einzig vorstellbare und richtige – aber eben nur Berliner – Antwort auf die Herausforderungen der Zeit, die an diese Stadt gestellt wurden. Etwas anderes war eben doch nicht möglich.

Noch ist er nicht fertig, und somit ist letztlich jede Beschreibung und Bewertung seiner Architektur vorübergehend und vorläufig. Und vieles ist eine Frage des Geschmacks. Niemand wird abstreiten, daß ein Ensemble entstanden ist, das belebt ist und besucht wird, an dem gearbeitet und eingekauft wird und wo man sich wieder amüsiert – keinesfalls subtil –, sondern in cleanen Kinocentern, im Musicaltheater, einer Spielbank oder eben bei McDonald's. Sein Mythos scheint ungebrochen, was auch immer er in seiner Geschichte war, ob Weltstadtkreuzung oder Karnickeloase, ob Baustelle oder wie heute ein Ort, an dem problemlos jedes beliebige Ereignis an scheinbarer Weltläufigkeit gewinnt. Wieder wird er bestaunt und fotografiert. Und es werden Bücher über ihn geschrieben. Es scheint, als stehe der Potsdamer Platz heute – wie schon in den 20er Jahren – für das Versprechen von Metropole in einer Stadt, die sich ihrer weltstädtischen Bedeutung wieder und wieder vergewissern muß. Und wir Berliner werden – gleich welches Urteil wir über ihn fällen, ob wir ihn mögen oder nicht – mit ihm leben (müssen), wir werden ihn lieben (lernen) und am Ende werden wir – wie zu allen Zeiten – jeden Besucher der Stadt eben an den Potsdamer Platz führen und ihm stolz das neue Berlin zeigen. Erklären kann man das wirklich nicht.

Jochen Visscher

lack of knowledge about the city. Here, they find a bit of everything and everyone – and everything is easy to confuse.

Its construction was an experiment. Where else were there such opportunities for planning an inner-city completely from scratch within a developed European capital? Quality was supposed to be guaranteed by important investors and famous architects who took on the redesigning. The result raises questions. Did the architecture succeed, or was an opportunity wasted? Is it daring, or conventional? Is it just megalomania, or maybe really the only conceivable and correct answer to the demands placed on this city – but precisely just an answer specific to Berlin? Nothing else was possible, after all. The square still isn't finished, so that every description and evaluation of its architecture is temporary and provisional. After all, it's a matter of taste. No-one will deny, however, that an ensemble has arisen that is lively, which people visit, or where they work and shop and enjoy themselves once more. This is by no means in a subtle way, but in clean cinema complexes, in musical theatres, in the casino, or just at McDonald's. Its legend seems to be unbroken. This is regardless of whatever it was in its history – metropolitan junction, rabbit oasis, building site or, as today, a place where every arbitrary event easily gains in seeming cosmopolitanism. Once again, it is being marvelled at and photographed. Books are written about it. It seems as if today, as already in the twenties, Potsdamer Platz stands for the promise of a metropolis in a city which must remind itself of its cosmopolitan importance over and over again. And irrespective of whatever judgement we may reach about it, whether we like it or not, we Berliners will live with it (or have to). We will love it (or learn to). And in the end, we will, as always, take all visitors to the city expressly to Potsdamer Platz and proudly show them the new Berlin. It really isn't something you can explain.

Jochen Visscher

Hans Wilderotter

Die Gegend vor dem Potsdamer Tor

Zur Geschichte des Platzes und seiner Umgebung

Der Potsdamer Platz verdankt seine Entstehung der Stadterweiterungspolitik der preußischen Kurfürsten und Könige. Im letzten Drittel des 17. Jahrhunderts wurde westlich der Berliner Festungsmauer die Dorotheenstadt nördlich der Straße Unter den Linden angelegt, südlich davon die Friedrichstadt, deren westliche Begrenzung die Mauerstraße bildete. Nach der vollständigen Besiedlung dieser beiden landesherrlichen „Privatstädte" veranlaßte König Friedrich Wilhelm I. (1713–1740), der sogenannte „Soldatenkönig", im Jahre 1732 die Erweiterung der Friedrichstadt nach Westen. Die Eckpunkte dieser Erweiterung bildeten drei Plätze, die am Ende der verlängerten Hauptachsen der Friedrichstadt angelegt wurden: das Rondell (ab 1814 Belle-Alliance-Platz, heute Mehringplatz) an der Friedrichstraße, das Quarré (ab 1814 Pariser Platz) an der Straße Unter den Linden und das Octogon (ab 1814 Leipziger Platz) an der Leipziger Straße.

Bis 1740 war der durch die Erweiterung notwendige Neubau der Stadtmauer fertiggestellt, durch die das Brandenburger Tor am Quarré, das Hallesche Tor am Rondell und das Potsdamer Tor am Octogon Einlaß in die Stadt boten. Diese Mauer hatte vor allem fiskalische Funktion. An den insgesamt dreizehn Toren wurde die Akzise erhoben, eine Verbrauchssteuer auf Waren des alltäglichen Bedarfs, die in der Mitte des 17. Jahrhunderts in Preußen eingeführt worden war.

Vor dem Potsdamer Tor zweigte die Landstraße nach Potsdam, die „Allée von Potsdam" hieß, nach Südwesten ab. Im spitzen Winkel dazu verlief nach Nordwesten eine Straße, die das Potsdamer Tor mit jener Landstraße verband, die in Verlängerung der Straße Unter den Lin-

Outside Potsdam Gate

The History of the Square and its Surroundings

Potsdamer Platz arose as a consequence of the urban expansion policy of the Prussian Electors and Kings. In the last third of the 17th century, Mauerstrasse marked the western limit of the Berlin fortress wall. As part of this expansion, the new city districts of Dorotheenstadt and Friedrichstadt were then layed out to the north and south of the road Unter den Linden respectively. By 1732, both these royal "private towns" were completely settled. As a result, King Frederick William I (1713–1740), nicknamed the "soldier king", ordered that Friedrichstadt be expanded westwards. Three squares layed down at the end of the extended principal axes of Friedrichstadt formed the cornerstones of this expansion. These were the Rondell (from 1814, Belle-Alliance-Platz, now Mehringplatz) on Friedrichstrasse, the Quarré (since 1814, Pariser Platz) on Unter den Linden, and the Octogon (since 1814, Leipziger Platz) on Leipziger Strasse.

This expansion meant that the city wall had to be built anew. It was completed by 1740. Entry to the city was now possible via Brandenburg Gate at the Quarré, Halle Gate at the Rondell, and Potsdam Gate at the Octogon. The wall's function was foremost a fiscal one. Its thirteen gates were used for raising excise, a consumer tax on goods of everyday use introduced in Prussia in the middle of the 17th century.

The country road to Potsdam branched off towards the south west in front of Potsdam Gate. It was called the "Allée von Potsdam". At an acute angle to the north west ran a road linking Potsdam Gate with the country road forming the extension of Unter den

den zum Schloß Charlottenburg führte. Diese Verbindungsstraße wurde ab Ende des 18. Jahrhunderts zum neu errichteten Schloß Bellevue durchgeführt und deshalb seit 1831 Bellevuestraße genannt.

Der „Platz vor dem Potsdamer Tor", wie er seit der Jahrhundertmitte bezeichnet wurde, ergab sich aus der Notwendigkeit, Raum für den Rückstau der auf Zollabfertigung wartenden Transportfahrzeuge zur Verfügung zu stellen. Dieser Stauraum war hier um so notwendiger, als der Verkehr zwischen der königlichen Sommerresidenz in Potsdam und der Hauptstadt erheblich war und durch den Handel mit der sächsischen Messestadt Leipzig noch gesteigert wurde, zu der eine Abzweigung von der Landstraße nach Potsdam führte, eine Tatsache, die der Leipziger Straße ihren Namen gegeben hatte. Der Ausbau und die Befestigung der „Allée von Potsdam" um 1792, ihre „Chaussierung", wie man damals sagte, gab ihr nicht nur den neuen Namen Potsdamer Chaussee, sondern auch einen klaren Hinweis auf ihre überragende Verkehrsbedeutung.

Vom Naherholungsgebiet zum Millionärsviertel

Zwischen der Potsdamer Chaussee, dem südlichen Rand des Tiergartens im Norden und dem Schafgraben, dem späteren Landwehrkanal im Süden, hatten seit Ende des 17. Jahrhunderts Angehörige der französischen Kolonie Berlins Gärtnereien angelegt. Als in der zweiten Hälfte des 18. Jahrhunderts der Tiergarten, der bis 1740 eingezäunt und den Mitgliedern der Hofgesellschaft vorbehalten war, für die Berliner Bevölkerung zum Naherholungsgebiet wurde, erweiterten einige Gärtner ihr Obst- und Gemüseangebot um einen Getränkeausschank für Ausflugsgäste. Aus diesen Provisorien entwickelten sich veritable Gartenlokale, von denen einige – *Der Hofjäger* und *Kempers Hof* auf dem Gelände des ehemaligen *Richardschen Kaffeegartens* – noch Anfang des 19. Jahrhunderts erheblich ausgebaut wurden. Darüber hinaus errichteten zahlreiche Gastwirte und Gärtner auf ihren Grundstücken

Linden and linking it with Charlottenburg Palace. This connecting road was built through to the newly-built Bellevue Palace from the end of the 18th century, and has thus been called Bellevuestrasse since 1831. The square had been known as the "Square in front of Potsdam Gate" since the middle of the century. It developed from the need to make space available for the transport vehicles waiting in the tailback for the customs post. This tailback area here was even more necessary since traffic between the Royal Summer Residence in Potsdam and the capital was considerable. It was increased still further by trade with the Saxonian fair town of Leipzig. A branch from the country road to Potsdam went off towards the latter, thus giving Leipziger Strasse its name. Around 1792, the "Allée von Potsdam" was extended and reinforced. Its macadamization, or *Chaussierung* as it was called in German at the time, didn't just give it its new name of Potsdamer Chaussee, but also a clear indication of its overwhelming importance in terms of traffic.

From Recreational Area to Millionaires' Quarter

Since the end of the 17th century, members of Berlin's French colony had established nurseries between Potsdamer Chaussee, the southern edge of Tiergarten Park to the north, and the sheep ditch, later the Landwehr Canal, to the south. Tiergarten Park itself had been fenced in until 1740 and reserved for members of court society. When it became a recreational area for the Berlin population in the second half of the 18th century, some gardeners expanded their range of fruit and vegetables with a bar for excursion guests. Some of these makeshift arrangements developed into real beer gardens, several of which were considerably expanded and built up as recently as the start of the 19th century. These included *Der Hofjäger*, and *Kempers Hof* on the premises of the former *Richardschen Kaffeegarten*. Beyond this, numerous landlords and gardeners erected

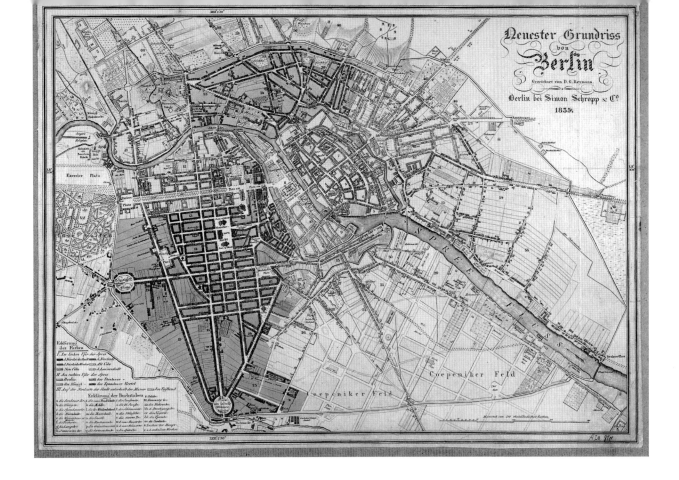

schmale und langgestreckte, eingeschossige Häuser mit kleinen, zumeist aus zwei Zimmern und einer Küche bestehenden Wohnungen, in denen sich Berliner Familien während des Sommers einmieten konnten.

Die Entwicklung zur Landhauskolonie wurde jedoch vor allem durch den Bau aufwendiger Sommerhäuser bestimmt, deren Eigentümer Angehörige der bürokratischen, kulturellen und ökonomischen Elite Berlins waren, und zu deren Erbauern nicht nur Maurermeister, sondern führende Architekten zählten. Bereits 1799 errichtete Friedrich Gilly ein Landhaus für den Geheimen Kriegsrat Mölter und im folgenden Jahr entwarf Carl Gotthard Langhans, der Erbauer des Brandenburger Tores, ein Haus für den Direktor des Berliner Nationaltheaters August Wilhelm Iffland, das zu den ersten Häusern gehörte, die ganzjährig bewohnt und deshalb repräsentativ ausgestattet wurden.

Damit war die Entwicklung von der Landhauskolonie zum Villenvorort eingeleitet, die ab dem dritten Jahrzehnt des 19. Jahrhunderts durch die Anlage neuer Straßen beschleunigt

long and narrow one-storey houses on their plots of land with small flats, mostly consisting of two rooms and a kitchen, in which Berlin families could take lodgings during the summer.

Development towards a country house colony was, however, primarily determined by the construction of extensive summer houses belonging to Berlin's bureaucratic, cultural and economic elite. Their constructors didn't just include master masons, but also leading architects. As early as 1799, Friedrich Gilly constructed a country house for the secret military advisor Mölter. In the following year, Carl Gotthard Langhans, constructor of the Brandenburg Gate, designed a house for the Director of the Berlin National Theatre, August Wilhelm Iffland. It was one of the first houses inhabited all-year-round and was correspondingly prestigiously equipped.

This marked the start of the development from a country house colony into a fashionable residential suburb. The process gathered momentum from the third decade of the 19th

Neuester Grundriß von Berlin, gezeichnet von D. G. Reymann, Berlin bei Simon Schropp & Co., 1835.

Newest ground plan of Berlin, drawn by D. G. Reymann, Berlin by Simon Schropp & Co. (ed.), 1835.

wurde. Ab 1836 wurde auf dem Gelände des Gartenlokals *Kempers Hof* eine Privatstraße angelegt, die auf die Kreuzung der Tiergartenstraße mit der Bellevuestraße mündete. In den beiden folgenden Jahrzehnten wurden unter anderem die Matthäikirchstraße und die Viktoriastraße angelegt, die jeweils von der Tiergartenstraße bis zum Landwehrkanal reichten, wo die Viktoriastraße, deren nördlicher Teil die ehemalige Privatstraße Kempers Hof war, auf die Potsdamer Straße traf. Die Matthäikirchstraße bildete in der Mitte ihres Verlaufs eine platzartige Erweiterung aus, auf der Friedrich August Stüler 1844–1846 die St. Matthäus-Kirche errichtete. Quer zur Viktoriastraße verlief die Margarethenstraße, die erst 1874 bis zur Matthäikirchstraße einerseits, 1914 zur Potsdamer Straße andererseits durchgelegt werden konnte.

Die Grundstücke an diesen Straßen und an der Bellevue- und Lennéstraße wurden parzelliert und mit zwei- bis dreigeschossigen freistehenden Villen und herrschaftlichen Mietshäusern bebaut, deren äußeres Erscheinungsbild im Stil des Berliner Klassizismus der Schinkelschule ein hohes Maß an Geschlossenheit aufwies, die sich nicht nur der fast gleichzeitigen Entstehungszeit verdankte, sondern auch der Tatsache, daß zum Beispiel in der Viktoriastraße der Architekt Friedrich Hitzig für fast 50 % der Häuser die Entwürfe zeichnete. „So ist", heißt es 1877 in *Berlin und seine Bauten*, „ein außerordentlich anmutiges Stadtviertel entstanden, wie es ähnlich kaum eine zweite Großstadt aufzuweisen hat."

„Die Gebäude selbst", heißt es an der gleichen Stelle, waren „mit breiten, wohlgepflegten Vorgärten versehen" und „entweder für die Benutzung einer einzelnen Familie bestimmt, oder doch auf Mieter aus den begütertsten und gebildetsten Klassen der Bevölkerung berechnet." Diese Familien – zu denen, um nur einige Beispiele zu nennen, der Bildhauer Friedrich Drake, die Brüder Wilhelm und Jacob Grimm und der Dichter Joseph von Eichendorff, vor allem aber Bankiers wie Hansemann, Bleichröder, von Schwabach und Fürstenberg gehörten, de-

century onwards when new roads were layed down. From 1836 on, a private road was layed down on the premises of the *Kempers Hof* beer garden, linking it with the junction of Tiergartenstrasse and Bellevuestrasse. In the next two decades, other roads followed, including Matthäikirchstrasse and Viktoriastrasse. The northern section of the latter was the former private road Kemper's Hof. Both roads stretched from Tiergartenstrasse to the Landwehr Canal, where Viktoriastrasse met up with Potsdamer Strasse. Matthäikirchstrasse formed a square-like extension half way along where Friedrich August Stüler constructed the St. Matthäus-Kirche in 1844–1846. Perpendicular to Viktoriastrasse ran Margarethenstrasse. This was only able to cut through to Matthäikirchstrasse on the one side and Potsdamer Strasse on the other in 1874 and 1914 respectively.

The plots on these roads, Bellevuestrasse and Lennéstrasse, were parcelled and built on with two to three-storey detached villas and grand apartment buildings. Their external appearance exhibited a considerable extent of consistency in the Berlin Classicist style of the Schinkel School. It is not just due to their almost simultaneous creation dates, but also to the fact that for example in Viktoriastrasse, the architect Friedrich Hitzig was responsible for designing almost 50 percent of all the houses. In 1877, the book *Berlin und seine Bauten* (Berlin and its Buildings) described it as follows: "In this way … an extraordinarily graceful urban district arose, one hardly matched by any other big city."

The book goes on: "The buildings themselves were equipped with broad, well-cared for front gardens" and "either intended for use by an individual family, or really calculated for tenants from the most affluent and educated classes of the population." Residents included, to name just a few examples, sculptor Friedrich Drake, philologist and folklorist brothers Wilhelm and Jakob Grimm, and poet Joseph von Eichendorff. But it was primarily thanks to bankers like Hansemann, Bleich-

Friedrich Hitzig:
Das Wohnhaus Drake, 1842.

Friedrich Hitzig:
Villa Drake, 1842.

nen die Gegend den Namen „Millionärsviertel" verdankte – hatten hier ihren Wohnsitz im Rahmen dessen genommen, was der „Zug nach Westen" genannt wurde, der im letzten Jahrhundertdrittel immer weiter führte, über Charlottenburg, den „Neuen Westen", schließlich bis in die Villenkolonie Grunewald. An diesem weiteren Zug beteiligten sich auch viele Bewohner des „Alten Westens", wie die Gegend vor dem Potsdamer Tor jetzt genannt wurde; freiwerdende Häuser und Grundstücke wurden von Botschaften, Behörden und Verbänden übernommen, so daß sich eine Mischnutzung entwickelte, die dem Gebiet etwas von seiner vornehmen Schläfrigkeit nahm. Gleichwohl konnte noch 1919 ein Journalist schreiben, man habe in dieser Gegend das Gefühl, „zugleich in Berlin und nicht in Berlin zu sein. Überall gehen noch lebendige Biedermeiergeister um, und ein edler, später, aber stilfeiner Klassizismus grüßt mit Giebeln, Säulen und Karyatiden."

Ein Touristenzentrum:
Bahnhof, Hotels und Restaurants

Auf der anderen Seite der Potsdamer Chaussee, die seit 1831 Potsdamer Straße hieß, wurden ab 1846 die Link-, Eichhorn- und Schellingstraße angelegt und mit vierstöckigen Mietshäusern ohne Vorgarten geschlossen bebaut. Es entstand ein Wohnviertel für gehobene Ansprüche, dessen Wohnqualität zwar hinter der des Millionärsviertels zurückblieb, aber als bevorzugtes Wohngebiet für höhere Beamte durchaus großen Prestigewert besaß, der in der Bezeichnung „Geheimratsviertel" nicht ohne Ironie zum Ausdruck kam. In diese Bebauung war die Ostseite der Potsdamer Straße einbezogen, während sich auf der Westseite noch weit über die Jahrhundertmitte hinaus eine ganze Reihe der Gärtnereien, Gartenlokale und Landhäuser halten konnte, die so charakteristisch für den Anfang des Jahrhunderts waren. Ab 1860 entstanden im Verlauf weniger Jahre durch Umbau oder Abriß und Neubau vierstöckige städtische Mietshäuser, in deren Erdgeschoß Ladengeschäfte eingebaut wurden. Die Potsdamer Straße entwickelte sich zur Geschäftsstraße.

röder, von Schwabach und Fürstenberg that the area owed its name of "Millionaires' Quarter". All of these had taken up residence here as part of what was known as the "journey west". This continued ever further in the last third of the 19th century, via Charlottenburg and the "New West" before finally getting as far as the villa suburb of Grunewald. Participants in this extended movement also included many residents of the "Old West", as the area in front of Potsdam Gate was now known. The houses and properties left behind were taken over by embassies, authorities, and associations, leading to a mixed use development and thus removing some of the area's distinguished sleepiness. Nonetheless, in 1919 a journalist could still write that in this area one had the feeling of "simultaneously being in Berlin and not being in Berlin. All over, still-lively Biedermeier spirits still circulate and a noble, late but stylish classicism beckons with gables, columns and caryatids."

A Tourist's Centre:
Railway Station, Hotels and Restaurants

In 1831, Potsdamer Chaussee was renamed Potsdamer Strasse. On the other side of this, Linkstrasse, Eichhornstrasse and Schellingstrasse were layed down and completely covered with four-storey apartment houses without front gardens. A residential district thus arose, one catering for elevated demands. Its living quality may not have matched that of the millionaires' quarter, but it certainly retained considerable prestige value as a preferred residential area for higher-level civil servants. This was expressed with a touch of irony in the label of "privy councillor quarter". The building did include the eastern side of Potsdamer Strasse, but on the western side, a whole row of nurseries, beer gardens and country houses, so typical for the start of the century, managed to last well into its second half. From 1860 onwards, urban blocks of rented flats four storeys high and with shops built into their ground floors arose in the

Diese Entwicklung verdankte sich vor allem dem „Zug nach Westen", der auch das Geschäftsleben erfaßt hatte, wurde aber erheblich beschleunigt durch die Tatsache, daß 1838 südlich des Potsdamer Platzes – mit diesem durch einen eigenen Vorplatz verbunden – der Potsdamer Bahnhof als Endpunkt der ersten preußischen Eisenbahnlinie von Potsdam nach Berlin eröffnet wurde. In dem Maße, in dem das Eisenbahnnetz ausgebaut und nationale und internationale Verbindungen hergestellt wurden, wuchs das Fahrgastaufkommen beträchtlich. Im Jahre 1890 sollen fast 1,5 Millionen Menschen am Potsdamer Bahnhof einen Zug bestiegen haben, und die Vermutung liegt auf der Hand, daß auch die Zahl derer, die hier einem Zug entstiegen, nicht kleiner war. Zur Bewältigung dieser Massen war 1868–1872 ein neues Bahnhofsgebäude in dem damals üblichen Stil eines Renaissancepalastes errichtet worden.

Dem neuen Bahnhof folgten die Hotels. In unmittelbarer Nähe und als Gelenkstelle zwischen Bahnhofsvorplatz, Potsdamer Platz und Leipziger Platz lag das *Hotel Fürstenhof*, das 1906/07 von der Firma Aschinger übernommen und erheblich umgebaut und erweitert

course of just a few years through reconstructing or tearing down and building anew. Potsdamer Strasse developed into a shopping street.

This development was mainly due to the "journey west" described earlier which also included business life. Moreover, it had been considerably speeded up by the fact that Potsdamer Bahnhof station was opened here in 1838 as the terminus of the first Prussian railway from Potsdam to Berlin. The station was south of Potsdamer Platz and linked with it via an own forecourt. Passenger numbers expanded so much that the railway network was expanded and national and international connections established. In 1890, almost one and a half million people are said to have boarded a train at Potsdamer Bahnhof, and it seems only logical to assume that there would have been a similar number getting out here as well. A new station building in the then usual style of a Renaissance palace was built between 1868 and 1872 in order to cope with these masses.

Hotels followed the new station. The *Hotel Fürstenhof* lay in the immediate vicinity and as a point of interaction between the station forecourt, Potsdamer Platz and Leipziger Platz. It had been taken over in 1906/07 by the *Aschinger* company and considerably rebuilt and expanded. Just opposite was the *Palast-Hotel*, built way back in 1892/93 on the north side of Potsdamer Platz, between Leipziger Platz on the one hand, and the northern part of Königgrätzer Strasse (the present day Ebertstrasse), on the other. Five years earlier still, the *Hotel Bellevue* had been built on the corner of Bellevuestrasse and Königgrätzer Strasse. The *Hotel Esplanade* must be mentioned in addition to all the smaller hotels and guest houses in the roads leading away from Potsdamer Platz. It was constructed in 1907/08 at 17–18a Bellevuestrasse by the so-called royal consortium, and expanded in 1911/12 into no. 16. The term corresponds with the hotel's luxurious furnishings and the exclusiveness of the guests.

Der Potsdamer Platz 1903. Blick in die Bellevuestraße (links) und die Königgrätzer Straße (rechts). Bildmitte: *Hotel Bellevue*, links die Terrasse des *Café Josty*.

Potsdamer Platz in 1903. View down Bellevuestrasse (left) and Königgrätzer Strasse (right). Centre: *Hotel Bellevue*, with *Café Josty* terrace to its left.

wurde. Gegenüber, an der Nordseite des Potsdamer Platzes, zwischen Leipziger Platz und Königgrätzer Straße, der heutigen Ebertstraße, war bereits 1892/93 das *Palast-Hotel* errichtet worden; vorausgegangen war, fünf Jahre zuvor, der Bau des *Hotels Bellevue* an der Ecke Bellevue- und Königgrätzer Straße. Neben all den kleineren Hotels und Pensionen in den Straßen, die aus dem Potsdamer Platz herausführten, muß vor allem das *Hotel Esplanade* genannt werden, das 1907/08 in der Bellevuestraße 17–18a, mit einer Erweiterung 1911/12 in der Nr. 16, von dem sogenannten Fürstenkonsortium errichtet wurde, eine Bezeichnung, die der luxuriösen Ausstattung des Hotels und der Exklusivität der Gäste entsprach. Im *Esplanade* kamen auf 600 Gästebetten 180 separate Badezimmer, ein Verhältnis, das weit über dem damals üblichen Durchschnitt lag. Nicht mitgerechnet sind die 60 Zimmer für die mitreisende Dienerschaft der Gäste, zu denen auch Kaiser Wilhelm II. gehörte, der hier seine Herrenabende zu veranstalten pflegte.

Neben den Hotels sorgte vor allem eine wachsende Zahl von Cafés und Restaurants dafür, daß die Gegend zum Anziehungspunkt für Touristen wurde. Zentraler Anlaufpunkt für Paare und Passanten, für Verliebte, Flaneure und Geschäftsleute, war das *Café Josty*, das 1880 an der Einmündung der Bellevuestraße auf den Potsdamer Platz eröffnet wurde und von dessen Terrasse man einen guten Überblick über das Treiben auf dem Platz hatte. Von den älteren Restaurants hatte *Frederichs Weinstube* in der Potsdamer Straße 12 die illustresten Gäste, unter ihnen der Maler Adolph von Menzel, der 1871–1876 in der Potsdamer Straße 7, und Theodor Fontane, der von 1873–1898 schräg gegenüber in der Nr. 134 c wohnte, nur wenige Meter vom *Weinhaus Huth* entfernt, das 1871 seine Pforten in Nr. 139 geöffnet hatte. Zwei Häuser weiter lag die *Konditorei Telschow* direkt am Potsdamer Platz. Sie zog 1909 in das benachbarte Eckhaus zur Linkstraße um, da 1909/10 an ihrem alten Standort das *Bierhaus Siechen* gebaut wurde, das spätere *Pschorr-Bräu-Haus.*

It had 180 separate bathrooms for its 600 guest beds, a proportion far above the then average. However, that figure doesn't even include the 60 rooms for servants travelling with the guests. Kaiser Wilhelm II was among the latter. He was in the habit of holding his gentlemen's evening parties here.

The area became a magnet for tourists. It was not just the hotels mentioned which were instrumental in this, but also the growing number of cafes and restaurants. *Café Josty* was the principal calling point for pairs and passers-by, for couples, strollers and businessmen. It was opened in 1880 at the junction of Bellevuestrasse and Potsdamer Platz. From its terrace, there was a good overview of the hustle and bustle on the square. *Frederichs Weinstube* at 12 Potsdamer Strasse had the most illustrious guests of the older restaurants. These included the painter Adolph von Menzel, who lived at 7 Potsdamer Strasse from 1871 to 1876, and Theodor Fontane, the poet, novelist, and essayist, who lived diagonally opposite at 134c from 1873 to 1898. Fontane lived just a few metres down from *Weinhaus Huth*, which had opened up at no. 139 in 1871. *Konditorei Telschow* lay two houses further on, directly on Potsdamer Platz. In 1909, it moved into the house next door, on the corner of Linkstrasse. This was to make way for *Bierhaus Siechen* (later the *Pschorr-Bräu-Haus*) which was built on the cafe's former site in 1909/10.

Bierhaus Siechen was not the first of the huge restaurants to open on Potsdamer Platz at that time. *Weinhaus Rheingold* was built back in 1906/07 at 19/20 Bellevuestrasse, between the *Hotel Esplanade* on the one side, and *Café Josty* on the other. It also belonged to Aschinger. However, its luxurious furnishings exceeded everything hitherto. The clear allusion to Richard Wagner's operas in the name was confirmed in the external form and the internal furnishings. The art historian Paul Westheim could still remember in exile in 1936 that in the *Nibelungensaal* and in the *Wotansaal* "a Wagnerian 'synthesis of the arts' had been stylized ... with Old Germanic

Der Potsdamer Platz, um 1930. Von links nach rechts: *Hotel Fürstenhof, Haus Vaterland,* Potsdamer Bahnhof und *Pschorr-Bräu-Haus,* in der Mitte der Verkehrsturm.

Potsdamer Platz around 1930. From left to right: *Hotel Fürstenhof, Haus Vaterland,* Potsdamer Bahnhof station and *Pschorr-Bräu-Haus,* in the centre: the traffic tower.

Das *Bierhaus Siechen* war nicht das erste der Riesenrestaurants, die um 1910 am Potsdamer Platz eröffnet wurden. Bereits 1906/07 war in der Bellevuestraße 19/20, zwischen *Hotel Esplanade* einerseits und *Café Josty* andererseits, das *Weinhaus Rheingold,* ebenfalls von Aschinger, errichtet worden, dessen luxuriöse Ausstattung alles bisherige übertraf. Die bereits im Namen deutliche Anspielung auf die Opern Richard Wagners wurde in der äußeren Gestaltung und der inneren Ausstattung bestätigt.

decorative sculptures in which the petty bourgeois could feast on pickled cabbage and knuckle of pork at a moderate price". Westheim went on to say that the French journalist Jules Huret had once described this "New Valhalla" as a "cathédrale de Wurst".
Haus Potsdam east of Potsdamer Bahnhof station was just as impressive as the *Rheingold.* It was constructed in 1910/11 by Franz Schwechten, the architect of Anhalter Bahnhof station and the Kaiser William Memorial

16

Der Kunsthistoriker Paul Westheim erinnerte sich noch aus dem Exil 1936, daß im *Nibelungensaal* und im *Wotansaal* „mit altgermanischem Plastikschmuck ... ein Wagnersches ‚Gesamtkunstwerk' stilisiert" worden sei, „ in welchem sich der Kleinbürger zu mäßigem Preis an Sauerkohl und Eisbein laben konnte"; der französische Journalist Jules Huret, so Westheim weiter, habe dieses „Neu-Walhall" einmal „cathédrale de Wurst" genannt.

Das *Haus Potsdam*, das von Franz Schwechten, dem Architekten des Anhalter Bahnhofs und der Kaiser-Wilhelm-Gedächtniskirche 1910/11 östlich des Potsdamer Bahnhofs errichtet wurde, stand mit seinem *Café Picadilly* im runden Kopfbau an der Stresemannstraße, das mit Sitzplätzen für 2500 Gäste das größte Café der Welt gewesen sein soll, dem *Rheingold* in nichts nach. Nach Beginn des Ersten Weltkriegs wurde das Café allerdings und mit ihm das ganze Haus aus patriotischen Gründen in *Haus und Café Vaterland* umbenannt und wurde schließlich nach Übernahme und Umbau durch die Firma Kempinski ab 1928 zum „kulinarischen Völkerkundemuseum", in dem sich Touristen nach der Ankunft am Potsdamer Bahnhof sofort vergnügen konnten. Die verschiedenen Abteilungen des Hauses waren als Rheinterrasse und Wildwestbar, als spanische Taverne und österreichisches Heurigenlokal, als ungarische Bauernschänke, türkisches Café und vieles andere mehr folkloristisch ausstaffiert. Von der Rheinterrasse ging der Blick auf ein Rheinpanorama, vor dem regelmäßig ein künstliches Gewitter aufzog. „Donner grollen, Blitze zucken", heißt es über dieses mechanische Naturwunder, über das der Reim kursierte: „Haus Vaterland macht alles gründlich, im Vaterland gewittert's stündlich", im Programm, das erklärte, der Besucher solle beim Betreten der Wildwestbar „die ganze Romantik des wilden Räuberlebens der großen schweigsamen Prärie" empfinden; in der ungarischen Bauernschänke dagegen „rollt das Blut heißer in den Pulsen, hier sagt man mit rassigem Frohsinn immer wieder Ja zum Leben, das sieghaft auch über graue Steppen jagen muß wie die feurigsten Ungarhengste".

Church. It's round top end on the southern part of Königgrätzer Strasse (now Stresemannstrasse) contained the *Café Piccadilly*, said to be the world's largest café with seating for 2,500 guests. However, the café, and with it the whole house, was renamed for patriotic reasons after the First World War had started. It was now called *Haus und Café Vaterland*. After the war, the building was eventually taken over by the Kempinski company and developed into a "culinary museum of ethnology" from 1928 onwards. Here, tourists could amuse themselves immediately after arriving at Potsdamer Bahnhof station. The house had numerous sections each fitted out in a folkloric manner: from a Rhine wine garden to a Wild West bar, a Spanish tavern to an Austrian wine bar, a Hungarian village inn to a Turkish café, and much more besides. The Rhine wine garden looked out over a panorama of the River Rhine whilst an artificial thunderstorm developed in front of it. There was even a popular rhyme about this mechanical natural wonder: "Haus Vaterland macht alles gründlich, im Vaterland gewittert's stündlich" (Haus Vaterland does things thoroughly, in Vaterland it thunders hourly). The programme described how "thunder rumbles – lightning flashes" and explained that on entering the Wild West bar, the visitor should feel "the whole romance of the wild robber life of the large silent prairie". In the Hungarian village inn, by contrast, "blood rolls hotter in the veins, here they say yes to life over and over again with vivacious and hot-blooded cheerfulness and also have to hunt across the grey steppes confident of victory like the fieriest Hungarian stallions".

From Tailback Area to Metropolis

It was a long journey from a tailback area in front of Potsdam Gate to a traffic junction in the centre of Berlin. However, Potsdamer Platz remained what it had been from the beginning: "no square", as Franz Hessel concluded in 1929, "but instead what is known

Situations-Plan von der Haupt- und Residenz-Stadt Berlin und Umgegend auf Grundlage des früheren Seneck'schen Planes, bearbeitet von W. Liebenow, 1867.

Site plan of the capital and residence city of Berlin and its surroundings, based on the earlier plan by Seneck, revised by W. Liebenow, 1867.

Karl Friedrich Schinkel: Entwurf für das Potsdamer Tor und den Potsdamer Platz, 1823.

Karl Friedrich Schinkel: plan for Potsdam Gate and Potsdamer Platz, 1823.

Vom Stauraum zum Weltstadtplatz

Es war ein weiter Weg vom Stauraum vor dem Potsdamer Tor zum Verkehrsknotenpunkt im Zentrum Berlins. Der Potsdamer Platz blieb allerdings, was er von Anfang an war, „kein Platz", wie Franz Hessel 1929 festhielt, „sondern das, was man in Paris einen *Carrefour* nennt, eine Wegkreuzung, ein Straßenkreuz, wir haben kein rechtes Wort dafür."

Am Anfang des 19. Jahrhunderts hatte Karl Friedrich Schinkel verschiedene Pläne vorgelegt, mit denen die Kreuzung die Form eines Platzes erhalten hätte. Im Jahre 1815 entwarf er einen gotischen Dom als Denkmal für die Befreiungskriege, für den als Bauplatz der Leipziger Platz – wie das Octogon nach der entscheidenen Schlacht in diesen Kriegen seit dem Vorjahr hieß – mit dem nach Westen erweiterten Potsdamer Platz zu einer langgestreckten Ellipse verbunden werden sollte. Dieser Plan blieb ebenso unausgeführt wie ein weiterer Plan Schinkels, den er 1823 vorlegte und in dem er vorschlug, ein neues Tor einige Meter in östlicher Richtung versetzt zu errichten und die dadurch vergrößerte Fläche vor dem Tor als kreisrunden, durch Grünanlagen gegliederten Platz anzulegen.

Verwirklicht wurden, nach Osten verschoben, nur die beiden Torhäuser in Form dorischer

in Paris as a *Carrefour* – a crossing of ways, a crossroads, an intersection. There is no proper word for it in German."

At the start of the 19th century, Karl Friedrich Schinkel presented various plans which would have given the intersection the form of a square. In 1815, he designed a Gothic Cathedral as a memorial for the German Wars of Liberation. A year previously, the Octogon had been renamed Leipziger Platz after the decisive battle in these wars. The cathedral's construction site was intended to link Leipziger Platz with Potsdamer Platz, now extended westwards, to form a long ellipse. The plan was never implemented. A similar fate was met by a further plan by Schinkel, presented in 1823, in which he proposed a new gate moved just a few metres eastwards. The thus increased area in front of the gate was to have been layed out as a circular space structured by green areas.

All that was implemented were the two gate houses in the form of Doric temples moved eastwards. They remained standing after the excise wall was torn down in 1867. The city had not long since expanded beyond this, and besides, it had also become superfluous following the switch to direct taxes. After the wall had been torn down, the two narrow streets on either side were combined to form a broad road. This was named Königgrätzer Strasse after the site of the decisive battle for

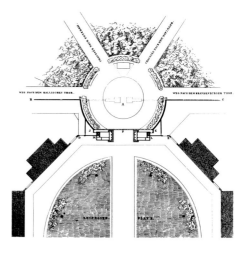

18

Tempel. Sie blieben stehen, als 1867 die Akzisemauer abgerissen wurde, über die die Stadt nicht nur längst hinausgewachsen, sondern die wegen der Umstellung auf direkte Steuern auch überflüssig geworden war. Nach dem Abriß konnten die beiden schmalen Straßen, die jeweils innerhalb und außerhalb der Mauer verliefen, zu einer breiten Straße zusammengefaßt werden, die Königgrätzer Straße genannt wurde, nach dem Ort der entscheidenden Schlacht im soeben für Preußen siegreich beendeten Krieg gegen Österreich.

Damit führte eine weitere zentrale Verkehrsachse über den Potsdamer Platz, die zur Steigerung des stetig wachsenden Verkehrs erheblich beitrug. Seit 1846 sorgten Pferdeomnibusse und seit 1879 Pferdebahnen, zusammen mit Fuhrwerken, Droschken, Handkarren und einer immer größeren Zahl von Fußgängern, für ein veritables Verkehrsgewühl auf dem Platz. Dessen Hauptursache war weniger die Zahl der Verkehrsteilnehmer als die Tatsache, daß alle den kürzesten Weg über den Platz suchten, so daß bereits Ende der 70er Jahre des 19. Jahrhunderts Theodor Fontanes General Poggenpuhl den Eindruck hat, daß die Pferdebahnen und Omnibusse „jeden Augenblick ineinander fahren wollten".

Was für den alten General aus der Sicherheit des Fensterplatzes im *Hotel Fürstenhof* ein Vergnügen war, wurde bereits 1895 als Bedrohung wahrgenommen. Hildegard Freifrau von Spitzemberg berichtet in ihrem Tagebuch, Bekannte „hätten sich anfangs gerührt umarmt, wenn sie nach solchem Übergange des Potsdamer Platzes sich gesund auf der Insel wiederfanden". In der Tat war das Verkehrsaufkommen inzwischen beträchtlich gewachsen, von vier Pferdebahnlinien, die den Platz im Jahre 1880 kreuzten, auf 13 Linien im Jahre 1897, um nach der Elektrifizierung zwischen 1898 und 1902 bis zum Jahr 1908 auf 35 anzusteigen. Ähnliche Zuwachsraten hatten auch die anderen Verkehrsmittel zu verzeichnen, wobei neben den Gütertransport und den öffentlichen Personennahverkehr zunehmend der Individualverkehr trat, der aber bis in die

Prussia in the just-finished victorious war against Austria.

One consequence of this was that another key traffic route now crossed Potsdamer Platz, leading to a considerable increase in the continuously growing traffic there. Since 1846 and 1879 respectively, horse-drawn buses and horse-drawn trams, along with horses and carts, cabs, hand carts and an ever greater number of pedestrians, ensured a true traffic turmoil on the square. The main cause of this was not so much the number of road users, but more the fact that everyone was looking for the shortest route across the square. The consequence was there for all to see – even in the novels of the time. Theodor Fontane gives an example of this from as early as the end of the 1870's: looking out of the window of the *Hotel Fürstenhof*, his General Poggenpuhl gained the impression that the horse-drawn buses and omnibuses "were any moment to drive into one another".

However, what might have been entertaining for the old general from the safety of his window seat, was already perceived as a threat by 1895. Hildegard Freifrau von Spitzemberg reported in her diary that "at first", acquaintances "hugged each other in a moved manner if they found each other again on the island uninjured after such a crossing of Potsdamer Platz". Indeed, in the meantime, the volume of traffic had increased considerably. Horse-drawn tram routes crossing the square increased in number from four in 1880 to 13 in 1897. This number increased still further to 35 in 1908 after the trams had been electrified between 1898 and 1902. Other means of transport also exhibited similar growth rates. Individual transportation played an increasing role in this process, alongside goods' transport and the dominant local public transport. However, right into the middle of the 20th century, this was still largely by bicycle.

But the feeling of being threatened by the traffic was increasingly being replaced by one of being fascinated by it. The first decade

Havestadt & Contag, Bruno Schmitz, Otto Blum: Entwurf zur Umgestaltung des Potsdamer Platzes, 1908–1910.

Havestadt & Contag, Bruno Schmitz, Otto Blum: plan for redesigning Potsdamer Platz, 1908–1910.

Brüder Luckhardt und Alfons Anker: Entwurf für die Westseite des Potsdamer Platzes, Photomontage 1932. Bildmitte: *Haus Berlin*, rechts: *Columbushaus*.

Brothers Luckhardt and Alfons Anker: plan for the western side of Potsdamer Platz, photomontage from 1932. Centre: *Haus Berlin*, right: *Columbus-Haus*.

Mitte des 20. Jahrhunderts noch weitgehend per Fahrrad erfolgte.

An die Stelle des Gefühls der Bedrohung trat jedoch zunehmend die Faszination durch den Verkehr. Im ersten Jahrzehnt des 20. Jahrhunderts beginnt die Veröffentlichung eines scheinbar endlosen Reigens von Feuilletons und Aufsätzen über den Potsdamer Platz, der jahrzehntelang nicht mehr abreißt und dessen Ergebnisse sich wie ein Ei dem anderen gleichen. Als Beispiel mag hier ein Text von Paul Westheim aus dem Jahre 1929 genügen, dessen Wortwahl unzweideutig die Begeisterung erkennen läßt, die er mit den anderen Autoren ähnlicher Artikel teilt: „Wie da von allen Seiten die Verkehrsströme heranbrausen, die Elektrischen, die Autos, die hastend nach ihren Ziel hingepeitschten Menschen, wie sich das immerfort verknäult und wieder entwirrt, anschwillt und abebbt, wie das wogt und reibt und flutet und sich nie erschöpft."

of the 20th century marks the start of the publication of a seemingly endless shower of feature articles and essays about Potsdamer Platz. Their results were as alike as two peas and the shower was to continue unceasingly for decades. A text by Paul Westheim from 1929 should suffice as an example. The choice of words unambiguously reveals the enthusiasm he shares with other authors of similar articles: "The streams of traffic roar inwards from all sides with the "electrics", the cars, and the people all being whipped towards their aim. How it tangles up and then unravels over and over again, swelling up and then fading away. How it surges and friction develops, streaming and never becoming exhausted."

Nevertheless, it would be correct to assume that the real traffic is relatively unimportant here. It is much more the enthusiasm for traffic in view of the wish to live in a city which can compare itself with other metropolises. This becomes clear in a text by Kurt Tucholsky written three years before Westheim's. He emphasizes that "The Berlin press is in the process of drumming in a new *idée fixe*: the traffic. Is it really so big? No. If you come to Berlin, lots of people ask you with a facial expression that almost pleas: "Isn't it true, the Berlin traffic is really colossal?" Now, I have found, that at its peaks, it roughly corresponds with the traffic in a medium-sized Parisian road at 6 o'clock in the evening – and that is very average, but nothing more. Moreover, where this childish fussing around is concerned, I have to say, that I cannot comprehend an attitude of mind impressed by the quantity of traffic. At some times of the day, there are six rows of cars standing next to each other at the Place de l'Opéra. So what? Does that raise Paris? Is Paris more valuable as a result? Now Berlin doesn't have this sort of traffic, but imagines that it does." Another author, Franz Hessel, reached a short and sweet conclusion about Potsdamer Platz in 1929: "Officially, the traffic is so colossal and in such an exceedingly confined space, that

Daß der Eindruck nicht ganz falsch ist, es käme hier gar nicht so sehr auf den tatsächlichen Verkehr an, sondern vielmehr auf die Begeisterung für den Verkehr angesichts des Wunsches, in einer Stadt zu leben, die sich mit anderen Weltstädten vergleichen kann, wird aus einem Text von Kurt Tuchosky deutlich, der bereits drei Jahre zuvor festhielt: „Die Berliner Presse ist dabei, dem Berliner eine neue fixe Idee einzutrommeln: den Verkehr. Ist er denn so groß? Nein. Kommst Du nach Berlin, so fragen Dich viele Leute mit fast flehendem Gesichtsausdruck: ‚Nicht wahr, der Berliner Verkehr ist doch kolossal?' Nun, ich habe gefunden, daß er an seinen Brennpunkten etwa dem Verkehr einer mittleren Pariser Straße abends um sechs Uhr entspricht – und das ist ein rechtes Mittelmaß, aber nicht mehr. Und gegenüber diesem kindlichen Getobe muß ich sagen, daß ich eine Geisteshaltung nicht begreife, der die Quantität eines Verkehrs imponiert. An der Place de l'Opéra stehen zu manchen Tagesstunden sechs Reihen Automobile nebeneinander – nun, und? Hebt das Paris? Wird Paris dadurch wertvoller? Nun hat Berlin diesen Verkehr nicht, bildet sich aber ein, ihn zu haben." Und Franz Hessel stellte 1929 über den Potsdamer Platz kurz und knapp fest: „Der Verkehr ist hier offiziell so gewaltig auf ziemlich beengtem Raum, daß man sich häufig wundert, wie sanft und bequem es zugeht."

Dafür sorgte seit 1924 der Verkehrsturm, die erste Ampelanlage Europas, ein acht Meter hoher Metallturm, der aussah, als habe man einen fünfeckigen Kiosk auf Stelzen gepackt, und der nicht genau in der Mitte der großen Kreuzung am Rande einer elliptischen Rasenfläche stand, die eine rudimentäre Form des Kreisverkehrs auf dem Platz einführte. Zusätzlich zu den Signallampen dieses Turms, der in der Presse wiederum als Beweis für den ungeheuren Verkehr auf dem Potsdamer Platz dargestellt wurde, regelten auch weiterhin Polizisten den Verkehr, da man sich nicht sicher war, ob die Lichtsignale tatsächlich beachtet würden. Die Aufstellung dieses Turms war die vorläufig letzte einer Reihe von Maßnahmen, die

one often wonders how gently and comfortably everything happens."

Since 1924, this was due to the traffic tower put up on the square – Europe's first set of traffic lights. This eight-metre high metal tower looked as if someone had packed a five-cornered kiosk on stilts. It stood not quite in the middle of the large junction on the edge of an elliptical lawn, introducing a rudimentary form of roundabout on the square. The tower's signal lamps were represented in the press as proof for the colossal traffic on Potsdamer Platz. They were aided by police who continued regulating the traffic since no-one was sure whether attention really would be paid to the light signal. The tower's construction was the last for the moment in a series of measures which were undertaken, or at least planned, since 1890 in regular intervals, in order to master the traffic on the square. It was necessary because the traffic really was substantial. Maybe not in comparison with Paris, or even the USA, which was continuously being used as a model and from where the traffic tower had also been imported. But it definitely was within the framework of the traffic otherwise normal in Berlin. The only

Martin Wagner: Entwurf zur Umgestaltung des Potsdamer Platzes mit dem „Verkehrskarussell", Modell 1929.

Martin Wagner: plan for redesigning Potsdamer Platz with the "traffic roundabout", model from 1929.

seit 1890 in regelmäßigen Abständen ergriffen oder zumindest geplant worden waren, um dem Verkehr auf dem Platz Herr zu werden. Denn dieser Verkehr war tatsächlich groß, zwar nicht im Vergleich zu Paris oder gar den Vereinigten Staaten, die immer wieder als Vorbild herangezogen wurden und von wo auch der Verkehrsturm importiert worden war, aber doch im Rahmen des sonst üblichen Verkehrs in Berlin, da der Straßenzug Leipziger Straße und Potsdamer Straße, neben dem Zug Unter den Linden und Charlottenburger Chaussee, der heutigen Straße des 17. Juni, die einzige Verbindung der alten Berliner Innenstadt mit den neuen Stadtteilen und mit den mit Berlin zusammenwachsenden Nachbarstädten im Westen und Südwesten war. Der Potsdamer Platz war ein Engpaß im Berliner Verkehr.

Ein letzter großer Plan zur Lösung der damit verbundenen Probleme wurde 1929 von dem Berliner Stadtbaurat Martin Wagner entworfen. Wagner wollte – ganz entsprechend seiner Theorie, daß ein Weltstadtplatz eine „fast dauernd gefüllte Verkehrsschleuse" sei – die Platzfläche vergrößern und in der Mitte des Platzes ein „Verkehrskarussell" mit 100 Metern Durchmesser bauen, um den Verkehr in drei Etagen zu leiten. Unter der Erde sollten die U-Bahnen fahren, das jetzige Straßenniveau sollte den Straßenbahnen und den Fußgängern vorbehalten bleiben und alle Kraftfahrzeuge in der ersten Etage fahren. In der zweiten Etage sollte ein großes Café eingerichtet werden mit einem Glasdach, aus dem am Abend das Licht über den Platz flutet. Dieses Licht hätte, wäre der Plan verwirklicht worden, das Blitzgewitter der Lichtreklamen, das am Abend über den Platz zuckte, noch erheblich verstärkt.

Ein erster Ansatz zur Verwirklichung des Plans wurde gemacht. Im Jahre 1928 begann der Abriß des *Hotels Bellevue*, um Platz zu machen für einen aus der bisherigen Bauflucht zurückgesetzten Neubau für die *Galeries Lafayette*. Das Haus, im Stil der Neuen Sachlichkeit entworfen von Erich Mendelsohn, wurde, nachdem die Verhandlungen mit dem Pariser Kaufhauskonzern gescheitert waren, als Bürogebäude

major routes connecting Berlin's old inner city and its new districts and the neighbouring towns growing together with it in the west and south west were Leipziger Strasse / Potsdamer Strasse and Unter den Linden / Charlottenburger Chaussee (the current Strasse des 17. Juni). Potsdamer Platz was a bottle neck in Berlin's traffic.

One last large plan for solving the problems linked with this was designed in 1929 by the Berlin municipal building surveyor Martin Wagner. Wagner's theory was that a square in a metropolis is an "almost continuously filled traffic floodgate". Following on from these ideas, he wished to increase the size of the square and build a 100-metre-wide traffic roundabout at its centre capable of leading the traffic to three different floors. Underground trains were to travel below ground. Trams and pedestrians were to be allocated the current street level. Motor vehicles were designated the first floor. A large café with a glass ceiling was to be installed in the second floor with light flooding out over the square in the evening. If the plan had been implemented, then this light would have considerably strengthened the storm of flashes from the neon signs flaring over the square in the evening.

One first attempt was made to implement the plan, however. In 1928, demolition of the *Hotel Bellevue* started so as to make room for a new building for *Galeries Lafayette,* set back from the hitherto line. The house was designed by Erich Mendelsohn in the contemporary functionalist style. It was built as an office building for another investor after negotiations failed with the Parisian department store company and, completely under the spell of the New World, was given the name *Columbus-Haus.* At around the same time, the Luckhardt brothers together with Alfons Anker designed a round skyscraper on the plot of *Café Josty* between the points where Potsdamer Strasse and Bellevuestrasse joined the square. *Haus Berlin*, designed by Luckhardt and Anker, was to be made completely out of

für einen anderen Investor errichtet und erhielt den Namen *Columbus-Haus*. Etwa gleichzeitig entwarfen die Brüder Luckhardt zusammen mit Alfons Anker, die bereits 1927 die Fassade des *Telschowhauses* an der Ecke Potsdamer und Linkstraße im modernen Stil umgestaltet hatten, ein rundes Hochhaus auf dem Grundstück des *Café Josty* zwischen den Mündungen der Potsdamer Straße und der Bellevuestraße, das *Haus Berlin*, das ganz aus Glas und Metall bestehen und durch üppige Leuchtreklame weithin Signale setzen sollte. Weder der Umbau des Platzes noch das *Haus Berlin* wurden verwirklicht.

Zentrum des NS-Regimes:
Der „Volksgerichtshof" und die
„Euthanasie-Zentrale"

Nach der Machtübergabe an die Nationalsozialisten im Januar 1933 änderte der Potsdamer Platz sein Gesicht kaum. Die dramatischen Veranderungen der Gegend betrafen vor allem die Belegung der Gebäude des ehemaligen Millionärsviertels, in die jetzt eine ganze Reihe von Dienststellen des NS-Staates und der NSDAP einzogen. Genannt werden muß vor allem der „Volksgerichtshof", der 1935 das Gebäude des ehemaligen Königlichen Wilhelms-Gymnasiums in der Bellevuestraße 15, neben dem *Hotel Esplanade*, übernahm, das 1863–1865 auf dem rückwärtigen Teil dieses Grundstücks errichtet worden war. Das Gymnasium, wenige Jahre zuvor für die immer größere Zahl der Schulpflichtigen aus dem Millionärsviertel gegründet, wurde 1921 geschlossen, da nach den grundlegenden Veränderungen der Gegend nicht mehr genügend Schüler angemeldet wurden; das Gebäude wurde bis 1935 vom Reichswirtschaftsrat genutzt. Der „Volksgerichtshof" war im Vorjahr als NS-Sondergericht gegründet worden, das unabhängig von dem üblichen Verfahrensrecht und auf der Grundlage nicht des Rechts, sondern der NS-Ideologie, buchstäblich „kurzen Prozeß" machte. In den zehn Jahren seines Bestehens (1934–1944) sprach das Gericht mehr als 12.000 Todesurteile; den bekanntesten Prozeß gegen die Attentäter des 20. Juli

glass and metal and blaze a trail for a long way through the opulent neon signs. *Telschowhaus,* on the corner of Potsdamer Strasse and Linkstrasse, had also had its facade altered in the modern style by the team back in 1927. In the end, the square was never rebuilt and *Haus Berlin* never constructed.

Headquarters of the Nazi Regime: the "People's Court" and the "Euthanasia Headquarters"

The face of Potsdamer Platz hardly changed after the transfer of power to the National Socialists in January 1933. The dramatic changes to the area primarily concerned occupancy of the buildings in the former millionaires' quarter by a whole number of offices of the Nazi state and Nazi Party. One building which must be identified here first and foremost is that of the "People's Court". In 1935 it took over the building of the former *Königliches Wilhelms-Gymnasium* at 15 Bellevuestrasse, next to the *Hotel Esplanade*. The school had been built on the rear part of the plot from 1863–1865. It was then closed in 1921, just a few decades after being established for the ever greater number of children required to attend school from the millionaires' quarter. There were simply not enough pupils registered following the fundamental changes to the area. The building was used until 1935 by the German Economic Council. The "People's Court" was founded in the year be-

Bauzaun Ecke Königgrätzer und Bellevuestraße, 1928. Geplanter Neubau eines Kaufhauses für die *Galeries Lafayette*; später *Columbus-Haus.*

Building site fencing at the corner of Königgrätzer Strasse and Bellevuestrasse, 1928. Planned new building of a department store for *Galeries Lafayette* (later *Columbus-Haus*).

fore as a Nazi special court. It literally made short work of its victims with quick trials independent of the usual law of procedure, based not on law but Nazi ideology. In the ten years of its existence (1934–1944), the court handed out more than 12,000 death sentences. The most infamous trial was that against the group which had attempted to assassinate Hitler on July 20th, 1944. That, though, was held in the former Court of Appeal in Kleistpark and presided over by Roland Freisler, President of the Court since 1942.

In 1940, the so-called "Euthanasia Headquarters" moved in just a few houses further down, at 4 Tiergartenstrasse, on the corner of Matthäikirchstrasse. This was known under an abbreviation derived from the address, "Aktion T4". It was set up in order to plan and implement the systematic mass murder of the mentally and physically disabled. The building had been constructed in 1890 as a villa for the banker Weissbach and was in possession of the Liebermann family since 1910. In 1940, it was taken over by the German Treasury as part of the systematic robbery of Jewish property described as "Aryanization". As an aside here, the policy of "Aryanization" was also visible on Potsdamer Platz, where in 1937, the Kempinski company's sign on *Haus Vaterland* was replaced by that of the F. W. Borchardt company.

The plan to transform Berlin into the "world capital Germania" would have had major consequences for the whole area. Indeed, in a particular way, it did. Albert Speer had been commissioned with its implementation in 1937 as the "General Building Inspector for the capital of the Reich". A seven-kilometre long and over 100-metre-wide "North-South Axis" was to stand in the centre of "Germania" as a magnificent boulevard. It was to have been lined with monumental buildings for the Nazi Party, the state and business. The axis was to be expanded to a "Runder Platz" 200 metres in diameter at the south end of its northern third, before it

Der Potsdamer Platz 1938. Blick in die Potsdamer Straße (links) und die Bellevuestraße (rechts). Rechts: *Columbus-Haus*, Bildmitte: *Hotel Esplanade*, links oben: das Gebäudes des „Volksgerichtshofs".

Potsdamer Platz in 1938. View down Potsdamer Strasse (left) and Bellevuestrasse (right). Right: *Columbus-Haus*, centre: *Hotel Esplanade*, top left: "People's Court" building.

1944, der allerdings im ehemaligen Kammergericht im Kleistpark stattfand, führte Roland Freisler, der seit 1942 Präsident des Gerichts war.

Nur wenige Häuser weiter, in der Tiergartenstraße 4 an der Ecke zur Matthäikirchstraße, nahm 1940 die sogenannte „Euthanasie-Zentrale" Quartier, die unter dem nach der Adresse benannten Kürzel „Aktion T 4" mit der Planung und Durchführung des systematischen Massenmords an geistig und körperlich Behinderten beauftragt war. Das Gebäude, 1890 als Villa für den Bankier Weißbach errichtet und seit 1910 im Besitz der Familie Liebermann, wurde 1940 im Rahmen des „Arisierung" genannten systematischen Diebstahls jüdischen Eigentums vom Reichsfiskus übernommen. Die Politik der „Arisierung" war übrigens auch am Potsdamer Platz sichtbar, wo 1937 am *Haus Vaterland* das Zeichen der Firma Kempinski durch das der Firma F.W. Borchardt ersetzt wurde.

Erhebliche Konsequenzen für die ganze Gegend hätte der Plan gehabt – und hatte sie in gewisser Weise auch – Berlin in die „Welthauptstadt Germania" umzugestalten, mit dessen Verwirklichung seit 1937 Albert Speer als „Ge-

neralbauinspektor für die Reichshauptstadt" beauftragt war. Im Zentrum „Germanias" sollte eine sieben Kilometer lange und über 100 Meter breite „Nord-Süd-Achse" als Prachtstraße stehen, die von monumentalen Gebäuden der Partei, des Staates und der Wirtschaft gesäumt worden wäre. Am Südende ihres nördlichen Drittels sollte diese Achse, vor dem Übergang über den Landwehrkanal, zu einem „Runden Platz" mit 210 Metern Durchmesser aufgeweitet werden, an dessen Rändern unter anderem die Zentrale der „Allianz"-Versicherung und ein „Haus des Fremdenverkehrs" errichtet werden sollte, das bis zur Einstellung aller Bauarbeiten im Frühjahr 1941 im Rohbau fertiggestellt war. Um den nötigen Bauplatz zu gewinnen, waren zuvor zahlreiche Häuser in der Viktoriastraße, der Margarethenstraße und der Potsdamer Straße abgerissen worden.

Zerstörungen: Das vorläufig letzte Kapitel

Weitere Zerstörungen des Gebietes waren Folge der alliierten Luftangriffe, denen schließlich viele Häuser am Potsdamer Platz und seiner näheren Umgebung zum Opfer fielen. Gleichwohl entfaltete sich bereits wenige Wochen nach Kriegsende reges Leben in den Trümmern. Der Potsdamer Platz wurde in den folgenden Jahren zum Zentrum des Schwarzmarktes, da hier der sowjetische, der englische und der amerikanische Sektor aneinandergrenzten und wenige Schritte über die Sektorengrenzen genügten, sich dem Zugriff der jeweiligen Polizeibehörden zu entziehen. In den unteren Geschossen von *Haus Vaterland*, die wie die Untergeschosse vieler Gebäude noch intakt waren, eröffnete eine HO-Gaststätte und im *Columbus-Haus* fand das Kaufhaus Wertheim, dessen Haupthaus am Leipziger Platz stark zerstört war, Unterkunft. Im *Weinhaus Huth* hatte eine kleine Weinstube geöffnet und vor dem *Pschorr-Bräu-Haus*, das nur wenig gelitten hatte, sollen 1946 bereits wieder einige der Blumenfrauen gestanden haben, die seit Jahrzehnten so charakteristisch für den Platz waren.

Ins Zentrum der Weltpolitik rückte der Platz am 17. Juni 1953, als es im sowjetischen Sek-

crossed the Landwehr Canal. Buildings intended to be built on the perimeter here included the headquarters of the Allianz Insurance group and a "House of Tourism". The shell of the latter was already complete when all construction work was halted in spring 1941. Numerous houses in Viktoriastrasse, Margarethenstrasse and Potsdamer Strasse had been demolished beforehand in order to obtain the required building site.

Destruction:
The last chapter, for the time being

The area suffered further destruction as a consequence of Allied air-raids with many houses on Potsdamer Platz and its immediate surroundings falling victim. Nonetheless, just a few weeks after the war ended, active life developed in the ruins. In the following years, Potsdamer Platz became the centre for the black market. This was because the Soviet, British and American sectors bordered each other here. Consequently, it took only a few steps across the sectoral boundaries to evade the respective police authorities. The lower floors of *Haus Vaterland* were still intact, like the lower floors of many buildings. An East German state restaurant moved in here, and the Wertheim department store found shelter in *Columbus-Haus*. Wertheim's main store on Leipziger Platz had been extensively destroyed. A small wine bar had opened in *Weinhaus Huth*, and it is said that as early as 1946, some women flower sellers which had been characteristic of the square for decades were already standing in front of the *Pschorr-Bräu-Haus* again.

The square moved into the centre of world politics on June 17th, 1953, as an uprising arose in the Soviet sector. This eastern half of the city had also functioned as the capital of East Germany since the two German states had been founded in 1949. In the uprising, the workers protested against the increases in labour norms without any increase in pay. Amongst other things, they marched down Leipziger Strasse to Potsdamer Platz,

tor, der seit der Gründung der beiden deutschen Staaten 1949 als Hauptstadt der DDR fungierte, zu einem Aufstand kam, bei dem Arbeiter gegen die Erhöhung der Arbeitsanforderungen bei gleichbleibendem Lohn protestierten und unter anderem die Leipziger Straße hinunter zum Potsdamer Platz zogen, wo im *Columbus-Haus* eine Dienststelle der DDR-Volkspolizei untergebracht war. Bei den gewalttätigen Auseinandersetzungen, in deren Verlauf übrigens die Polizisten im *Columbus-Haus* eine weiße Fahne hißten und nach West-Berlin flohen, gerieten das *Columbus-Haus* und das *Haus Vaterland* in Brand und wurden jetzt erst vollständig zerstört. Der Aufstand wurde durch Einsatz der Panzer der sowjetischen Besatzungsmacht mit Gewalt beendet.

Gleichwohl blieb es auch in den folgenden Jahren bei einem regen Grenzverkehr. Mit dem Bau der Mauer zwischen Ost- und West-Berlin im August 1961 jedoch war das Leben am Potsdamer Platz weitgehend beendet. Östlich der Mauer, die auf weiten Strecken ziemlich genau da verlief, wo hundert Jahre zuvor die Zollmauer gestanden hatte, wurden sämtliche Gebäude, die in ruinösem Zustand, zum Teil jedoch wiederaufbaufähig, erhalten geblieben waren, abgeräumt, um freies Blick- und Schußfeld für die Grenzbewachung zu haben.

Westlich der Mauer wurden etwa dort, wo die Potsdamer Straße auf den Potsdamer Platz mündete, Souvenirbuden aufgestellt für Touristen, die einen Blick auf, und, von einem eigens errichteten Podest, über die Mauer werfen wollten. Die meisten Häuser wurden hier bereits in den 50er Jahren abgeräumt, um über eine Vorbehaltsfläche für das Regierungsviertel einer zukünftigen gesamtdeutschen Hauptstadt zu verfügen. Bereits 1957 begann der Senat von Berlin mit dem Ankauf der Grundstücke im Gebiet um den Platz und ließ die noch bestehenden Gebäude abtragen. Im selben Jahr wurde der Plan gefaßt, eine als „Westtangente" bezeichnete Stadtautobahn in Nord-Süd-Richtung über den ehemaligen Potsdamer Platz zu führen, der erst 1981 aufgegeben wurde. Im vorläufigen Bebauungsplan aus dem Jahre

where an East German police station was housed in *Columbus-Haus*. During the violent clashes, the police in *Columbus-Haus* raised a white flag and fled to the western half of the city. Moreover, *Columbus-Haus* and *Haus Vaterland* both caught fire. Only now were they completely destroyed. The uprising was ended violently when the Soviet occupiers' tanks were deployed.

Nevertheless, border traffic remained lively in the following years too. However, for the most part, life at Potsdamer Platz ended after the Berlin Wall had been built between the two halves of the city in August 1961. For long stretches, it followed pretty much the course of the old excise wall a century earlier. East of it, all remaining buildings were cleared in order to give the border guards free fields of view and fire. The buildings were in a ruinous condition, but in part capable of being reconstructed.

West of the Wall, where Potsdamer Strasse joins Potsdamer Platz, souvenir kiosks were erected for tourists wishing to take a look at the Wall and over it from a platform put up specially for the task. Most houses on this side were already cleared in the 1950s as to have a reserve area available for the government sector of a future all-German capital city. As early as 1957, the Berlin city government started buying plots in the area around the square and had the buildings still standing torn down. In the same year, the plan was made to build the *Westtangente*, an urban motorway leading across the former Potsdamer Platz in a north-south direction, which was not abandoned until 1981. In the provisional construction plan from 1960, before the Wall was built, only the *Hotel Esplanade* is still marked as worth retaining.

After the Wall was built, it seemed obvious to abandon the use of the area for an all-German government sector. The already agreed decision to construct the *Philharmonie* according to plans by Hans Scharoun on the northern end of the former Viktoriastrasse, completed in 1963, offered occasion to place further cul-

Der Potsdamer Platz 1947. Rechts: Blick in die Potsdamer Straße, Mitte: *Pschorr-Bräu-Haus*, links ein Torhaus von Schinkel.

Potsdamer Platz in 1947. Right: view down Potsdamer Strasse, centre: *Pschorr-Bräu-Haus*, left: a gate house by Schinkel.

1960, also noch vor dem Bau der Mauer, ist nur noch das *Hotel Esplanade* als erhaltenswert verzeichnet.

Nach dem Bau der Mauer lag der Verzicht auf die Nutzung des Geländes für ein Regierungsviertel nahe. Der bereits zuvor gefaßte Beschluß, auf dem Nordende der ehemaligen Viktoriastraße die Philharmonie nach Plänen Hans Scharouns zu errichten, bot, nach Fertigstellung des Baus 1963, Anlaß für die Entscheidung, weitere Kultureinrichtungen an dieser Stelle zu plazieren. Für den Neubau der Nationalgalerie nach Plänen Ludwig Mies van der Rohes, der 1968 abgeschlossen war, wurde 1962/63 der immer noch bestehende Rohbau für das „Haus des deutschen Fremdenverkehrs" abgerissen. Für den Neubau der Staatsbibliothek von Hans Scharoun schließlich, die von 1967 bis 1978 errichtet wurde, wurde die Politik der Zerstörung der Stadtgestalt, der die Nationalsozialisten vorgearbeitet hatten, fortgesetzt mit der Verlegung der Potsdamer Straße, über deren südliches Ende zwischen der nicht mehr existierenden Margarethenstraße und dem Landwehrkanal der Neubau errichtet wurde, während die neue Trasse als innerstädtische Schnellstraße nach Westen verschoben wurde. Wie sehr es dabei auch um Entlastung von der Geschichte ging, wird deutlich an der Tatsache, daß genau unter dieser neuen Potsdamer Straße der größte Teil jenes Gebäudes verschwunden ist, in dem der nationalsozialistische „Volksgerichtshof" untergebracht war.

tural facilities at this spot. In 1962/63, the still existing shell for the "House of German Tourism" was torn down to make way for the New National Gallery, built according to plans by Ludwig Mies van der Rohe. The gallery was finished in 1968. Finally, the new building of the National Library by Hans Scharoun, built between 1967 and 1978, saw the continuation of the policy of destroying the area's urban form prepared by the Nazis. It was now continued with the rerouting of Potsdamer Strasse. The new building was constructed over its southern end, between the no longer existing Margarethenstrasse and the Landwehr Canal, whilst the new route was shoved westwards as an inner city expressway. How important the process of lessening the historical burden also was in this can clearly be seen by the fact that the major part of the building housing the National Socialist "People's Court" has disappeared under this new Potsdamer Strasse.

Blick vom Potsdamer Platz auf den Leipziger Platz und in die Leipziger Straße am 17. Juni 1953.

View from Potsdamer Platz down Leipziger Platz and Leipziger Strasse on June 17th, 1953.

Blick über die Mauer am Potsdamer Platz, 1972. Im Vordergrund *Hotel Esplanade* und Bellevuestraße.

View over the Wall at Potsdamer Platz, 1972. In the foreground *Hotel Esplanade* and Bellevuestrasse.

Roland Enke

Vertane Chancen?

**Städtebauliche Planungen und
Wettbewerbe für den Potsdamer Platz**

Als am 3. Oktober 1998 das debis-Areal am
Potsdamer Platz in weiten Teilen feierlich
eröffnet wurde, wirkungsvoll auf den Tag der
Deutschen Einheit gelegt, hatte nicht nur das
nach Bombenkrieg, Nachkriegsabrissen und
Mauerbau leergefegte Gelände wieder eine Gestalt erhalten, es war auch eine für europäische Verhältnisse beispiellose Aufgabe, ein
zentrales Stadtquartier inmitten einer Metropole gänzlich neu wiedererstehen zu lassen, in
kürzester Zeit bewältigt worden.

Schon 1990 begannen in Folge des Zusam-
menbruchs der DDR, dem Fall der Mauer und
der Wiedervereinigung beider deutscher Staaten die konkreten Überlegungen zur Neugestaltung dieser einstigen Nahtstelle, die
historisch nicht nur eine zwischen dem alten
Berlin mit dem strengen Straßenraster der
Friedrichstadt und dem westlich gelegenen,
aufgelockerten Kulturforum war, sondern auch
eine zwischen den zusammenwachsenden
Stadthälften von Ost- und West-Berlin ist. In
dieser Zeit, beflügelt durch die schier unend-
lichen Möglichkeiten, Ideen und Pläne zu
formulieren und gar zu verwirklichen, begann
eine leidenschaftliche Debatte über Architektur und städtebauliche Leitbilder, die an
die 20er Jahre und das vielbeschworene
„Laboratorium der Moderne" erinnerte. Obwohl der Potsdamer Platz in eben jener Zeit
im strengen Sinn nur eine hektische Verkehrs-
kreuzung war und als Un-Platz galt, wurde
er als Inbegriff des städtischen Fortschritts
beschworen. Und trotz des komatösen Zustan-
des, in dem der Potsdamer Platz nach dem
Zweiten Weltkrieg lange Zeit vor sich hin däm-
merte, geriet er zum Paradefall und Mittel-
punkt des neu zu schaffenden hauptstädtischen Lebens.[1]

Missed Opportunities?

**The Re-creation of Potsdamer Platz –
Planning, Competitions and Construction**

The inauguration of the debis development
at Potsdamer Platz was held, for symbolic effect, on 3 October, 1998, the Day of German
Unity. Swept clean by the bombs of World
War II, post-war demolition and the erection
of the Berlin Wall, this expanse of land had
in large part been given form once again. The
ceremony celebrated the rapid execution of
an unparalleled task: the re-creation, from
the ground up, of a central quarter in a European metropolis.

With the construction of the Wall in 1961,
Potsdamer Platz was robbed of its status as
bridge between the rigorous street grid of the
Friedrichstadt to the east and the looser
post-war plan of the Kulturforum to the
west. It now represents one of the primary
nodes at which East and West Berlin are
growing back together. 1990, following the
collapse of the GDR, the fall of the Wall and
the reunification of the two German states,
the first concrete steps were taken towards
the rebuilding of this former vital urban link.
The endless possibilities for the realisation of
this unprecedented opportunity ignited an
impassioned debate over architecture and
urban design models which recalled the
vaunted "laboratory of modernism" of the
nineteen twenties. Although the Potsdamer
Platz of that era was, strictly speaking, a
hectic intersection that hardly qualified as a
plaza, it was held up as the very embodiment
of urban progress. And, despite its long
period of dormancy through the decades
following the war, it re-emerged as the focal point of the capital's urbanistic aspira-
tions.[1]

During preparations for West Berlin's International Building Exhibition (IBA 1984/

In den späten 70er Jahren, während der Vorbereitungen zur Internationalen Bauausstellung „IBA 1984/1987", gewann unter dem Kernthema der Wiederentdeckung der Innenstadt als Wohnort auch der Bereich zwischen der südlichen Friedrichstadt, dem Potsdamer Platz, dem Tiergarten und dem Spreebogen wieder besondere Aufmerksamkeit. Das erklärte Ziel war die Rettung der „kaputten Stadt"; einerseits wurde damit der Stadtplanung der 50er und 60er Jahre, die fast ausschließlich auf Verkehrsplanung, eine hohe Gewerbedichte im Zentrum ausgerichtet war und im Wohnungsbau dem Leitbild der gelockerten Stadt folgte, eine vehemente Absage erteilt, andererseits wurden erste Grundlagen für den die kommenden Jahrzehnte prägenden Begriff der „Kritischen Rekonstruktion" von Berlin gelegt. Die Bezeichnung „Zentraler Bereich / Mitte" zwischen Reichstag und Landwehrkanal etablierte sich, es folgte die Wiederaufnahme städtebaulicher Verfahren, wobei die durch die IBA-Planungen angestoßene Diskussion 1981 von der neu geschaffenen Senatsverwaltung für Stadtentwicklung aufgegriffen wurde. Die folgenden Hearings, Gutachten und Rahmenpläne blieben zwar als Konzepte in der Schublade und in der Realität wurde weiter am Ausbau eines eigenständigen Stadtzentrums gearbeitet, dennoch aber erwuchs die Erkenntnis gerade für den Bereich des Potsdamer Platzes, daß die Stadtplanung auch auf eine mögliche Verknüpfung beider Stadthälften vorbereitet sein müßte. In der Folgezeit wurden vereinzelte Entwürfe veröffentlicht, die auch den Potsdamer Platz miteinbeziehen, die aber trotz der erkennbar visionären Inhalte ein Thema anrissen, das erst im Zuge der Wettbewerbe nach dem Mauerfall für Zündstoff sorgte: das Hochhaus. So fertigte Oswald Mathias Ungers 1983 Pläne für ein 200 Meter hohes Gebäude östlich der Staatsbibliothek; Helge und Margret Bofinger 1988 im Rahmen von „Berlin: Kulturstadt Europas" 751 Meter hohe Türme u. a. auf dem Leipziger Platz, die das Alter Berlins symbolisieren sollten.[2]

Die andauernde Suche, die mannigfaltigen Ideen und Vorschläge, die stets an der politi-

1987) in the late 1970s, the area comprised by the southern Friedrichstadt, Potsdamer Platz, the Tiergarten and the Spreebogen had gained special attention under the central theme "Rediscovering the Inner City". The stated aim was the rescuing of the "ruined city". Accordingly, the urban planning approach of the 1950s and 1960s – restricted to traffic engineering, central commercial density and an open model of housing development – was vehemently refuted. Further, the foundations were laid at this time for the city's "critical reconstruction", the concept that would ingrain itself in the planning discourse of the coming decades. "Central Area / Mitte" established itself as the designation for the area from the Reichstag to the Landwehrkanal. The urban design process resumed, and in 1981 the debate that had been spurred ahead by the IBA planning was taken up by the newly created Senate Administration for Urban Development. The outline plans that resulted from the subsequent hearings and reports remained in the drawer as concepts, while in reality work continued on the expansion of an independent city centre. Nonetheless, the recognition grew that, for the area around Potsdamer Platz in particular, planners should prepare for the eventuality of the rejoining of the city's two halves. During the period that followed, a number of individual design schemes involving Potsdamer Platz were published which, though clearly of visionary character, touched on a theme that would later fuel controversy in the series of competitions after the fall of the Wall: the skyscraper. These included Oswald Mathias Ungers' 1983 project for a 200-metre-high building to the east of the Staatsbibliothek, as well as 751-metre-high towers symbolising Berlin's age, for, among other sites, Leipziger Platz, conceived in 1988 by Helge and Margret Bofinger on the occasion of Berlin's celebration as "Cultural City of Europe".[2]

Following the failure of wide-ranging ideas and proposals due to the political realities in

schen Realität scheitern mußten, begann sich auf West-Berliner Seite im Frühjahr 1989 – also noch vor dem Mauerfall – konkreteren Planungen zuzuwenden, als sich die Rot-Grüne Koalition unter dem Bürgermeister Walter Momper anschickte, erste Gespräche über einen Grundstücksverkauf mit dem Daimler-Benz-Konzern zu führen. Vorrangigstes Ziel war es, durch Ansiedlung eines zahlungskräftigen Unternehmens der unterfinanzierten Stadt höhere Steuereinnahmen zu garantieren, Arbeitsplätze zu schaffen und dem Wandel von einer Industrie- zur Dienstleistungsgesellschaft zu begegnen. Nach dem zuerst in Augenschein genommenen Standort am Klingelhöfer-Dreieck am südwestlichen Tiergartenrand schälte sich alsbald das Gelände am Potsdamer Platz heraus.

Der Fall der Mauer schließlich schuf vollendete Tatsachen; im Juli 1990 wurde ein 68.000 m² großes Gelände von der Daimler-Benz AG erworben, ein Jahr später setzte der japanische Elektronikkonzern Sony seine Unterschrift unter den Kaufvertrag. Der geringe Kaufpreis des Daimler-Grundstückes von 92,9 Mio. DM wurde schnell als „Schnäppchen" bezeichnet; Bedenken des Berliner Landesrechnungshofes sowie der Europäischen Union in Brüssel, die dem Senat verdeckte Subventionen unterstellte, hatten zwar eine Nachzahlung von Daimler-Benz in Höhe von 33,8 Mio. DM zur Folge, jedoch blieb der Kaufpreis mit rund 1860 DM/m² weit unter den 20.000 DM, die beispielsweise mit einem Grundstück Unter den Linden erzielt wurden. An dieser Entscheidung wurde aber auch weitergehende, heftigste Kritik laut, in die unisono sowohl linke wie konservative Publizisten, Architektur- und Stadttheoretiker einstimmten: vom Ausverkauf der Stadt an Großinvestoren, gar dem Kniefall vor dem Kapitalismus war die Rede. Die Stadt beraube sich durch den Verkauf der Möglichkeiten, Funktionen, Nutzungen und Rahmenbedingungen vorzugeben: Das von Hoffmann-Axthelm favorisierte städtebauliche Leitbild, Vielfalt aus der Berlin-typischen, kleinteiligen Parzelle entstehen zu lassen[3], schien ebenfalls gescheitert.

the divided city, the ongoing planning search took a turn toward the concrete. In early 1989, even before the fall of the Wall, West Berlin's governing coalition of Social Democrats and Greens under Mayor Walter Momper took up talks with the Daimler-Benz corporation regarding a property deal. The administration's primary aims in trying to attract the concern to Berlin were to secure higher tax revenues for the financially strapped city, generate employment, and address the challenge posed by Berlin's shift from an industrial to a service-based economy. The negotiating parties initially focused on Klingelhöfer-Dreieck at the south edge of the Tiergarten as a potential location, until, a short time later, political developments thrust the Potsdamer Platz site to the fore.

With the fall of the Wall, the stage was finally set. In 1990 and 1991, respectively, the Daimler-Benz corporation and the Japanese electronics giant Sony both signed property deals with the city. Daimler-Benz acquired its 68,000-sqare-metre site for 92.9 million D-marks. The bargain price raised more than a few eyebrows. Misgivings on the part of the Berlin Auditor-General's Office, as well as the European Union in Brussels, which suspected the Berlin Senate of granting the automaker hidden subsidies, led to an additional payment by Daimler-Benz of 33.8 million D-marks. Still, the final purchase price per square metre worked out to around 1,860 D-marks, compared with 20,000 D-marks for properties on, for example, the city's central boulevard, Unter den Linden. The deal unleashed a storm of protest from journalists across the political spectrum, and from architectural and urban theorists who complained that the city was selling out to corporate interests, indeed even bowing to the forces of capitalism. These critics asserted that the city was surrendering its power to determine options, functions and conditions in the use of its own land. The urban design model advocated by Dieter Hoffmann-Axthelm – that of fostering variety through the

Befürchtet wurde, der Verkauf eines solch großen, innerstädtischen Geländes an wenige Investoren werde einseitigen Nutzungen Vorschub leisten, die Stadt veröden und aus dem Potsdamer Platz in absehbarer Zeit den „Potsdaimler Platz" machen. Auch wurde kritisiert, daß der zwar zähe, aber mühsam erarbeitete Demokratisierungsprozeß in Form von Bürgerbeteiligung und Fachdiskussionen der IBA bewußt außer Kraft gesetzt werde.

In das Vakuum, einen Zustand aus scheinbarer Hilflosigkeit und planerischem Stillstand, einerseits gefördert durch die Doppelherrschaft von Senat und Magistrat, andererseits durch den Wechsel vom Rot-Grünen Senat zur Großen Koalition von SPD/CDU nach der Wiedervereinigung beider Stadthälften, stieß Ende 1990 ein „Medienspektakel", bei der Massenmedien als Auftraggeber der Stadtgestaltung fungierten. Neben der Programmzeitschrift *TEMPO* und einer Sonderausgabe des populistischen Wissenschaftsmagazins *GEO,* die sich mit Visionen der künftigen Architektur Berlins beschäftigten, initiierten die Publizisten Wolf Jobst Siedler und Michael Mönninger eine Serie in der *Frankfurter Allgemeinen Zeitung.* Hier meldeten sich bekannte Feuilletonisten ebenso zu Wort wie 17 Architekten, die ihre Vorschläge zu Berlins Mitte zu Papier brachten. Zusammengefaßt wurden die Beiträge von Vittorio Magnago Lampugnani in einer Ausstellung des Deutschen Architektur Museums in Frankfurt.[4] Die Visionen von Zaha Hadid, Coop Himmelblau, John Hejduk und vieler anderer orientierten sich jedoch in keiner Weise an der historischen Struktur oder boten gar Lösungen der real anstehenden Probleme der Stadt Berlin. Die publizistische Resonanz war überwiegend ablehnend, die Entwürfe wurden als „reiner Kunstakt" und „Eintritt des Städtebaus ins postmoderne Medienzeitalter" bezeichnet[5], nur vereinzelt gab es Zustimmung, wenn auch leicht ironisierend: „es ist große sinnstiftende ästhetik herausgekommen, aber auch viel heiße luft des freien geistes."[6]

Es fanden sich aber zwei Architekten, an deren Vorschlägen sich in der Folgezeit eine

development of small lots in the Berlin tradition[3] – also seemed to have failed. It was feared that the sale of such a large, central area to just a few investors would result in one-sided use and a general urban monotony. The replacement of Potsdamer Platz by "Potsdaimler Platz" was seen as imminent. The critics further maintained that the democratisation of the planning process, hard won through public participation and IBA expert discussions, was being intentionally derailed. This state of moribund planning was encouraged on the one hand by the double-rule of the Senate and Magistrate and, on the other, through the transfer of power following the city's reunification, from the "red-green" Senate to the "great coalition" between the Social and Christian Democrats. At the end of 1990 the mass media plunged into this vacuum and effectively took up the reins in the planning process. The city magazine *Tempo* and the popular science journal *Geo* published special issues illustrating visions of Berlin's architectural future, while the journalists Wolf Jobst Siedler and Michael Moenninger ran a series in the *Frankfurter Allgemeine Zeitung* focusing on Berlin's central district, Mitte. Contributors to the FAZ series included well-known feature writers, as well as 17 noted architects, all of whom put forth their proposals for the district. Vittorio Magnago Lampugnani gathered these in an exhibition that was mounted by the German Architectural Museum in Frankfurt.[4] The visions of Zaha Hadid, Coop Himmelblau, John Hejduk and many of the others did not take into account Berlin's historical structure or, indeed, offer solutions to the practical problems confronting the city. The journalistic response was predominantly negative. The designs were criticised as "purely artistic gestures" and "urban design's entry into the post-modern media age".[5] Critical approval, where it was to be found at all, often carried an ambivalently ironic tone: "great and edifying beauty has come out of it, if also much hot air of the free spirit."[6]

heiße Debatte entzündete, die sich für Berlin als durchaus folgenreich herausstellen sollte.[7] Der bereits Mitte der 80er Jahre eröffnete Streit um die künftige Stadtgestaltung, verschlagwortet als „Provinz" mit parzellierter Kleinteiligkeit der Kritischen Rekonstruktion der Neubau-IBA auf der einen Seite, und der „Großstadtarchitektur", konkretisiert durch das Hochhaus als Versinnbildlichung der Metropole auf der anderen. Auf den ersten Blick schienen die Entwürfe eines Josef Paul Kleihues, der aus einer kompakten Blockstruktur östlich der Staatsbibliothek ein 250 Meter hohes Turmhauspaar entwickelte, oder eines Hans Kollhoff, der sowohl am Alexanderplatz wie am Potsdamer Platz einen Cluster von freistehenden Hochhäusern vorschlug, den Stadtraum an der Leipziger Straße aber in traditioneller Höhe ergänzte, einzig die Möglichkeit zu suggerieren, daß die Stadt für morgen nur mit Hochhäusern zu gestalten sei. Deutlich wurde jedoch, daß in beiden Entwürfen die anfänglich gegensätzlichen Positionen versöhnt wurden, und sich eine Synthese aus dem Leitbild einer europäisch inspirierten Stadt mit amerikanischen Einsprengseln gebildet hatte, durch die der Begriff der „Kritischen Rekonstruktion" neu belebt wurde.[8]

Die Vielzahl von Hochhausentwürfen jener Zeit verstärkten jedoch die Ablehnung von, wie es hieß, „stadtzerstörerischen Großformen". Die „Gruppe 9. Dezember" hatte bereits im Juli 1990 die „Charta für die Mitte von Berlin"[9] verfaßt, die unverkennbar die Handschrift des „Parzellenphilosophen" Dieter Hoffmann-Axthelm trug. Neben der Parzelle als grundlegendem Strukturelement sowie der Orientierung an überlieferten Ordnungsprinzipien wurde vor allem Funktionsmischung, soziale Vielfalt und Stadtökologie in den Vordergrund gestellt. Die unterschiedlichen Auffassungen, ja der Dissens zwischen Architektenschaft und Politik, dem die Senatoren Wolfgang Nagel (SPD, Bauverwaltung) und Volker Hassemer (CDU, Stadtentwicklung) durch konkurrierende Kompetenzansprüche und dem Vorrang politischer Entscheidungen beiläufig Vorschub leisteten,

However, there were two architects whose proposals sparked a heated debate over the ensuing months, one which would have consequences for the city.[7] A dispute had begun during the mid-1980s concerning Berlin's future form, in which the small-lot "critical reconstruction" of the IBA was labelled "provincial" by its detractors, who sought a "big city architecture" focused on the skyscraper as central symbol. Josef Paul Kleihues envisioned a pair of 250-metre-high towers rising from a compact block structure east of the Staatsbibliothek. Hans Kollhoff proposed clusters of free-standing high-rises for both Alexanderplatz and Potsdamer Platz while maintaining the traditional building height for the area around Leipziger Strasse. At first glance, such designs seemed to suggest that skyscrapers constituted the single and indispensable solution to the city of tomorrow. A closer look made clear, though, that both Kleihues' and Kollhoff's designs reconciled the originally opposing positions by embedding the occasional American element in a European-inspired model, thus forming a synthesis which brought new vitality to the concept of "critical reconstruction".[8]

This notwithstanding, the multitude of skyscraper designs conceived in this period served to intensify resistance to building forms that were perceived as "destructive to the city". In July 1990 the "Gruppe 9. Dezember" had published the "Charter for Berlin's Centre"[9], which bore the unmistakable handwriting of "small-lot philosopher" Dieter Hoffmann-Axthelm. Alongside the small land parcel as basic structural element and the orientation to traditional ordering principles, the manifesto placed special emphasis on functional mix, social diversity and urban ecology. The dissent between the architectural profession and the political establishment, which was only spurred on by the competing claims of authority of Senators Wolfgang Nagel (SPD, Building Construction) and Volker Hassemer (CDU, Urban Develop-

mündete in der Forderung nach einem unabhängigem Senatsbaudirektor. Die Berufung von Hans Stimmann (SPD) im Mai 1991 entsprach jedoch in keiner Weise dem Wunsch der Architekten, da Stimmann als Vertreter der behutsamen Stadterneuerung angesehen wurde, als konservativ galt und „Baron Haussmann unserer Tage"[10] tituliert wurde. Um dennoch die Architekten einzubinden wie auch die öffentliche Meinungsbildung positiv zu beeinflussen, hatte Stadtentwicklungssenator Hassemer im April 1991 das Stadtforum als Diskussions- und Beratungsplenum ins Leben gerufen.[11]

Am 28. Juni 1991 schrieb die Senatsverwaltung für Stadtentwicklung und Umweltschutz den lange erwarteten, internationalen städtebaulichen Ideenwettbewerb für den Potsdamer Platz / Leipziger Platz aus, der aber auf Architekten beschränkt blieb und somit de facto alle Stadtplaner von dem Verfahren ausschloß. Nach einem Bewerberverfahren, an dem sich rund 75 Architekturbüros beteiligt hatten, folgte die Einladung von nur 16 Teilnehmern; die anfängliche Mißstimmung wurde so von heftigen Protesten abgelöst, an deren Spitze sich die Berufsverbände Bund Deutscher Architekten BDA und die Berliner Architektenkammer stellten. Der Architekten- und Ingenieursverein zu Berlin AIV initiierte am 1. Juli 1991 eine unbeschränkte, offene städtebauliche Ideenkonkurrenz unter Architekten, Stadt- und Landschaftsplanern, die, von wenig Resonanz begleitet, im Spätherbst im Martin-Gropius-Bau der Öffentlichkeit präsentiert wurde.[12]

Die Ausschreibung war bereits im Sommer 1990, noch im Sinne eines ökologischen Stadtumbaus unter der Stadtentwicklungssenatorin Michaele Schreyer (Die Grünen), formuliert worden, ehe durch die Senatsumbildung der Amtsnachfolger Hassemer das Verfahren an sich zog; auch auf den ersten Sitzungen des Stadtforums wurde über die Planungen am Potsdamer Platz diskutiert, die teilweise Eingang in den Wettbewerb gefunden haben. Die städtebaulichen Zielvorstellungen sprachen dezidiert

ment), resulted in the demand for an independent Senate building commissioner. The appointment of Hans Stimmann (SPD) to this position in May 1991 in no way reflected the wish of the architectural profession; Stimmann was viewed as a representative of "gentle urban renewal", as conservative, and as the "Baron Haussmann of our day"[10]. In order to involve architects in the process as well as positively influence public opinion, Urban Development Senator Hassemer had called the "Stadtforum" into being as discussion and advisory forum.[11]

On 28 June, 1991, the Senate Administration for Urban Development and Environmental Protection announced the long-awaited international urban design competition for Potsdamer and Leipziger Platz. The competition was limited to architects, thus excluding urban planners from the process. Following an application phase involving around 75 architectural firms, just sixteen were invited to participate in the competition itself. Initial discontent grew into vociferous protest led by the professional architectural associations, the Association of German Architects and the Berlin Association of Architects. On 1 July, 1991, the Berlin Association of Architects and Engineers (AIV) initiated an unlimited, open urban design competition for architects, landscape architects and urban and regional planners. The submitted concepts were exhibited in the Martin-Gropius-Bau in late autumn of that year, to only muted public reception.[12]

The competition guidelines had been formulated in summer 1990 under Urban Development Senator Michaele Schreyer (the Greens) in accordance with ecological urban redevelopment principles, before the Berlin Senate was reorganised and Schreyer's successor, Hassemer, took up the helm. Planning considerations for Potsdamer Platz were also debated at the first meetings of the Urban Forum, some of which found their way into the design competition. The urban design objectives conceived of Potsdamer Platz neither as

davon, den Potsdamer Platz weder als neue und einzige Mitte zu entwickeln, noch die Leitvorstellungen eines Citybandes zwischen Alexanderplatz und Kurfürstendamm wiederzubeleben, sondern das Neubaugebiet in die polyzentrische Stadtstruktur einzubinden, die auf die Bildung Groß Berlins 1920 sowie die Herausbildung der beiden Zentren nach dem Mauerbau zurückzuführen war.[13] Eine breite Nutzungsmischung sollte erzielt werden, um der Monofunktionalität des Kulturforums entgegenzuwirken. Ein urbaner Charakter war gefordert, der einerseits durch die Abfolge von Straßen und Plätzen zum Flanieren und Verweilen, andererseits durch das Beibehalten der wesentlichen Merkmale der Berliner Innenstadt – geometrischer Stadtgrundriß und geschlossene Blockränder – erreicht werden sollte. Zentraler Bestandteil bildete die Wiederherstellung der Raumfolge Potsdamer – Leipziger Platz: Während der Potsdamer Platz räumlich klar definiert werden mußte, sollte der Leipziger Platz eine Gestalt erhalten, die ihn als großstädtischen Platz mit stadthistorischem Wert auswies. Der Begriff „Parzellenstruktur" wurde dahingehend definiert, daß er als Ausgangspunkt für eine funktionale und gestalterische Nutzung verstanden werden kann, also Hotel neben Theater und nicht: Theater im Hotel. Die angestrebte Dichte sollte auf ihre Verträglichkeit überprüft und, ebenso wie die Höhenentwicklung, mit den tatsächlichen Nutzungen und im Sinne einer „Architektur für den einprägsamen Ort" formuliert werden. Weiterhin war die Optimierung des Stadtklimas ein Thema, wobei die Gelände des Lenné-Dreiecks und des ehemaligen Potsdamer Bahnhofs als Grünflächen zur Verfügung standen. Das öffentliche Nahverkehrsnetz (U- und S-Bahn sowie ein neuer Regionalbahnhof) sollte ausgebaut, der Individualverkehr massiv beschränkt werden. Schließlich mußten historische Denkmäler wie das *Weinhaus Huth,* das *Hotel Esplanade,* der Wurmfortsatz der alten Potsdamer Straße integriert und die Staatsbibliothek durch einen neuen Eingang zur alten Potsdamer Straße mit dem Potsdamer Platz verbunden werden.

single new city centre nor as revived part of an urban "band" stretching from Alexanderplatz to the Kurfürstendamm. Rather, they spoke of it expressly as a new development area to be integrated in the city's polycentric structure resulting from the administrative formation of "Greater Berlin" in 1920 and the formation of separate centres following the erection of the Wall.[13] A diversity of uses was called for to counter the functional homogeneity of the Kulturforum. An urban character was to be achieved through a sequence of pedestrian-friendly streets and squares within a street plan that maintained the defining traits of Berlin's historic inner city – the regular streetfront development of geometrically shaped city blocks. The re-creation of the spatial sequence from Potsdamer to Leipziger Platz was made a central component of the planning guidelines. Whereas Potsdamer Platz had to be given clear spatial definition, Leipziger Platz was to be reconstructed to reflect its historical status and form. Accordingly, the term "small parcel structure" was taken as departure point in a functional and design sense; i.e., hotel next to theatre, not theatre in hotel. The desired density was to be examined for its viability and, like the development in terms of height, was to be formulated with the foreseen uses in terms of an "architecture for the memorable place". The optimisation of the urban climate was a further aim, for which the Lenné-Dreieck and the area of the former Potsdamer railway station were available as green space. Means of public transport (underground, light rail and a new regional railway station) were to be expanded and automobile traffic strictly limited. Finally, guidelines called for the integration of historic landmarks such as the *Weinhaus Huth,* the *Hotel Esplanade* and the tail-end of the old Potsdamer Strasse, and the connection of the Staatsbibliothek to Potsdamer Platz by way of a new entrance from the old Potsdamer Strasse.

On 1 and 2 October, 1991, the competition entries were assessed and the Munich archi-

Modellaufnahme des
1. Preises von Hilmer &
Sattler im städtebaulichen
Wettbewerb Potsdamer und
Leipziger Platz, Oktober
1991.

Model, first-place entry by
Hilmer & Sattler in the
urban design competition
for Potsdamer and
Leipziger Platz, October
1991.

Am 1. und 2. Oktober 1991 wurden die Arbeiten begutachtet und der Siegerentwurf des Münchner Architektenduos Heinz Hilmer und Christoph Sattler bekanntgegeben, der die Beiträge von Ungers, Otto Steidle, William Alsop und Jan Störmer sowie Axel Schultes/ BJSS mit Charlotte Frank auf die Plätze verwies.[14] Ihr Entwurf war von einem räumlich komplexen, europäischen Stadtmodell geprägt, das von 35 Meter hohen kompakten Kuben und verdichteten Straßen gebildet wird. Große Solitäre der einzelnen Investoren sind nicht vorgesehen, sondern ein dichtes, städtisches Gewebe; bewußt wurde auch auf ein überdachtes Einkaufszentrum verzichtet. Der Potsdamer Platz erhält eine rechteckige Form und wird mit zwei 17geschossigen Ecktürmen als Torsituation sowie weiteren hohen Gebäuden umgeben; der Leipziger Platz wird in die historische oktogonale Gestalt zurückversetzt und von einer 10geschossigen Bebauung gesäumt. Die Verkehrserschließung erfolgt oberirdisch, Grünzüge am Lenné-Dreieck bzw. das als Wasserfläche gestaltete Bahnhofsareal verbinden den Tiergarten mit dem Südgelände am Gleisdreick.

Insgesamt folgte die Prämierung des Hilmer & Sattler Entwurfes den Vorgaben im Rahmen der „Kritischen Rekonstruktion" und „Berlinischen Architektur", die in der turbulenten Aufwärmphase 1990/91 diskutiert worden sind.

tectural team of Heinz Hilmer and Christoph Sattler declared the winners, defeating Ungers, Otto Steidle, William Alsop and Jan Störmer, and Axel Schultes/BJSS with Charlotte Frank.[14] Hilmer & Sattler's design was conceived on a spatially complex European urban model, formed of compact, 35-metre-high blocks on a dense street plan. Rather than large single buildings to be put up by the individual property owners, the design foresaw a dense urban fabric. A covered indoor shopping mall was intentionally omitted. Potsdamer Platz itself assumed the shape of a rectangle surrounded by two gate-like 17-storey corner towers and further high-rise buildings. Leipziger Platz was returned to its historic octagonal form and enclosed by ten-metre-high structures. Automobile traffic was to circulate at ground level. Green spaces at Lenné-Dreieck and a series of water basins on the former site of the railway station connected the Tiergarten with the south section at Gleisdreieck.

On the whole, the award of the top prize to Hilmer & Sattler was in step with the guidelines set out by the "critical reconstruction" and "Berlin architecture" as discussed in the turbulent warm-up phase of 1990/91. And it immediately released a new wave of indignation. Criticism of the competition results began when jury member Rem Koolhaas, having taken a pledge of secrecy, attacked Stimmann in an open letter for his authoritarian stance and refusal to consider farther-reaching impulses. Koolhaas went on to illuminate what he saw as the basic underlying dilemma – that Berlin was not up to the artistic and political demands of the task at hand and was thus doomed to succumb to a reactionary, provincial and amateurish urban conception.[15] The architectural as well as the general press echoed his arguments to a large extent, casting the Hilmer & Sattler plan as a small-town, least-common-denominator solution to the most important building commission of the decade.

The storm of protest against the jury and its decision resulted in the designs of the run-

Unmittelbar darauf erhob sich ein erneuter Sturm der Entrüstung. Die Kritik an den Wettbewerbsergebnissen eröffnete ein Mitglied der Jury, Rem Koolhaas. In einem offenen Brief attackierte er trotz Schweigepflicht nicht nur die autoritäre Haltung Stimmanns und sein Hinwegfegen von weiterführenden Denkanstößen, sondern das grundlegende Dilemma, daß Berlin dieser Aufgabe künstlerisch und politisch nicht gewachsen und deshalb dazu verurteilt sei, sich einem reaktionären, provinziellen und dilettantischen Stadtbegriff anzupassen.[15] Die Fach- und Tagespresse schlossen sich weitgehend dieser Meinung an und postulierten, daß mit dem Hilmer & Sattler Entwurf der kleinste gemeinsame Nenner gefunden und die wichtigste Bauaufgabe des Jahrzehnts wie eine Lokalangelegenheit behandelt wurde.

Die heftigen Angriffe auf die Jury und ihre Entscheidung hatten zudem zur Folge, daß die Entwürfe der weiteren Preisträger in der Öffentlichkeit kaum ernsthaft diskutiert wurden. Der zweite Preisträger Ungers, der mit seinem Entwurf den Vorgaben der Ausschreibung am nächsten kam, schlug ein rechtwinkliges, idealisiertes Raster vor, das sich an der kleinsten Blockgröße der Friedrichstadt orientiert; Ungers überlagert die historischen Straßenzüge und läßt so eine Struktur unterschiedlich großer, aber gleich hoher Blöcke entstehen. Ein drittes Raster, das Bezug auf die ehemalige Parzellenstruktur am Landwehrkanal nimmt, markiert mögliche Standpunkte von ergänzenden Hochhäusern. Auch der vierte Preis von Alsop & Störmer, der mit seinen futuristisch anmutenden Bauten, die sich sternförmig vom Leipziger Platz aus horizontal erstrecken und an ihrem westlichen Ende in vertikale Dominanten übergehen, den wohl modernistischsten Standpunkt verkörperte, fand kaum einen publizistischen Niederschlag. Unberücksichtigt blieben auch Kleihues, der mit zwölf 35geschossigen Hochbauten an der Westseite das Kulturforum vom Bebauungsgebiet abriegelte, und Kollhoff, in dessen Entwurf sieben Hochhäuser halbkreisförmig den

ners-up in the competition receiving scant public attention. The winner of the second prize, Ungers, who more fully than any other entrant satisfied the requirements of the design problem, proposed an idealised rectangular grid which took its dimensional cue from the Friedrichstadt's smallest block size. His plan overlies the historic street lines, thus creating a structure of city blocks of varying size but constant height. A third grid based on the former small-lot structure along the Landwehrkanal marked locations for the possible addition of high-rise buildings. The press also more or less ignored Alsop & Störmer's fourth-place entry, which, with its slightly futuristic buildings stretching out in a star formation from Leipziger Platz before rising vertically at their west ends, represented the most strongly modernist stance in the competition. Kleihues' design was similarly overlooked, with its twelve 35 storey towers on the west side of the site that effectively fenced the Kulturforum off from the new development. Kollhoff's concept received the same treatment, though his seven high-rise buildings in semi-circular formation around Potsdamer Platz it were seen as presenting the most truly convincing solution to the problem. The criti-

Lageplan des 2. Preises von O.M. Ungers im städtebaulichen Wettbewerb Potsdamer und Leipziger Platz, Oktober 1991.

Site plan, second-place entry by O.M. Ungers in the urban design competition for Potsdamer and Leipziger Platz, October 1991.

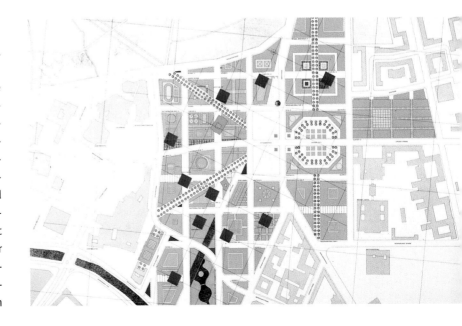

Potsdamer Platz umfangen und der als die eigentlich überzeugende Lösung angesehen wurde. Die Kritik wurde aber auch von Investorenseite kräftig geschürt: Diese waren an der Ausschreibung nur indirekt beteiligt gewesen und durften nur im Anhang ihre Vorstellungen vage äußern. Der Generalbevollmächtigte von Daimler-Benz, Matthias Kleinert, prägte die eingängige Formel, daß sich die Investoren gezwungen sähen, „für ein Niveau irgendwo zwischen Berlin und Posemuckel bauen zu müssen"[16]; Rainer Wagner, Geschäftsführer von Sony Berlin, verurteilte die „üblen Dogmen des 19. Jahrhunderts" und forderte „große, spektakuläre Architektur".[17]

Wie ein Damoklesschwert schwebte über dem Verfahren der Masterplan von Richard Rogers. Er war bekanntermaßen bereits im April von den Investoren Daimler-Benz, Sony, Hertie und ABB aufgrund seiner in London realisierten Bauten für Großinvestoren mit einem Gegenentwurf beauftragt worden. Am 20. Oktober 1991 wurde in der Ruine des alten *Hotel Esplanade* auf jener Veranstaltung, auf der der Senat gerade seine Preisträger präsentierte, buchstäblich durch die Hintertür der Entwurf von Richard Rogers effektvoll eingeführt. Finanziell üppig ausgestattet – dem mit 1,8 Mio DM vergüteten Entwurf standen 40.000 DM Preisgeld für Hilmer & Sattler gegenüber – ging Rogers von der Rekonstruktion des Leipziger Platzes aus, der ein kreisförmiger Potsdamer Platz folgt; Rogers beansprucht diesen Freiraum als *people's place* und Ort der Begegnung. Hier steht ein runder Turm, der den Zugang zu den unterirdisch liegenden Bahnstationen und zugleich das Zentrum der sich anschließenden sternförmigen Bebauung bildet. Die langgestreckten Baukörper schließen im Inneren jeweils eine überdachte Einkaufsstraße ein; am Potsdamer Platz wird die Traufhöhe von 22 Metern eingehalten, die langsam terrassenartig ansteigt und in Höhendominanten endet. In Nord-Süd-Richtung schlägt Rogers einen Autotunnel vor, ein Grüngürtel entlang der Ebertstraße über das Bahnhofsareal verbindet den Tiergarten mit dem Landwehrkanal.

cism was strongly echoed from the side of the investors, who had been involved only indirectly in drawing up the competition guidelines and allowed to make only a vague statement of their views in an appendix to the document. Daimler-Benz's legal representative, Matthias Kleinert, summarised the property owners' view of their position as "having to build at a level somewhere between Berlin and the backwoods."[16] Rainer Wagner, managing director for Sony Berlin, called for "great, spectacular architecture" and condemned the "evil dogmas of the nineteenth century."[17]

Richard Rogers' masterplan hovered over the process like a sword of Damocles. Due to his corporate buildings in London, he had been awarded a contract by Daimler-Benz, Sony, Hertie and ABB as early as April to conceive a counter-proposal to the official design selection. On 20 October, 1991, Rogers' design was literally slipped in, to great effect, through the back door of the ruin of the old *Hotel Esplanade* at the Senate's presentation of the winning competition entries. Amply rewarded at 1.8 million D-marks – in contrast to the 40,000 D-marks awarded Hilmer & Sattler – Rogers' design took as its starting point the reconstruction of Leipziger Platz along historical lines, followed by the adjacent Potsdamer Platz in circular form. Rogers conceived the plaza as a free "people's place" – a place of encounter. He placed a round tower here which served simultaneously as access to the underground transit stations and as focal point for connected homogeneous blocks of buildings radiating out, star-like, from the plaza. Each elongated block enclosed in its interior a covered shopping street. At Potsdamer Platz the buildings hold to a cornice height of 22 metres, then gradually rise, terrace-like, culminating in high, vertical structures. Rogers proposed a north-south tunnel for automobile traffic, while above, a strip of green space stretched from the Tiergarten, along Ebertstrasse, to the Landwehrkanal, taking in the former station area.

Modellaufnahme des von den Investoren am Potsdamer Platz beauftragten Beitrages von Richard Rogers für den Potsdamer und Leipziger Platz, Oktober 1991.

Model of Richard Rogers' design for Potsdamer and Leipziger Platz, commissioned by the property owners, October 1991.

Von der Fachpresse wurde der Entwurf hoch gehandelt; allein aber der Vorwurf, Rogers arbeite nur im Interesse der Investoren, die darüber hinaus mit dem Gegenentwurf noch den Senat düpierten, ließ eine ungeahnte politische Allianz entstehen, die zur Ablehnung des Entwurfes führte. Der Berliner Architekt Jürgen Sawade ging sogar so weit, ein Stadtverbot für den Kollegen zu fordern[18]. Rogers selbst sprach von der „schrecklichsten Erfahrung meines Lebens".[19] Um das Gesicht nicht zu verlieren, mußte der Senat, der durch den vorschnellen Verkauf die Malaise selbst verursacht hatte, auf der gefällten Entscheidung beharren, konnte jetzt ein letztes Mal Härte gegen die Allmacht der Investoren zeigen und erhielt über diesen Umweg nun auch die Zustimmung der Architektenverbände. Weiteren Einfluß übte er durch die strikten Gestaltungsvorgaben für den Leipziger Platz aus.

In den folgenden Monaten wurden an dem städtebaulichen Plan von Hilmer & Sattler einige Änderungen vorgenommen, der zur Grundlage des im März 1992 ausgeschriebenen Realisierungswettbewerbes für das Daimler-Areal gemacht wurde.[20] Gefordert war, das Grundstück als Bindeglied zwischen Kulturforum und Potsdamer Platz zu planen; die Traufhöhe wurde auf 35 Meter zuzüglich zweier zurückgesetzter Staffelgeschosse festgesetzt. Am Potsdamer Platz und am Landwehrkanal ist eine Bebauungshöhe von 80 Metern möglich. Erwogen wird auch ein Straßentunnel zur Erschließung sowie Ver- und Entsorgung. Eingeladen waren 14 Architekten; am 4. September 1992 wurde die Bürogemeinschaft von Renzo Piano und Christoph Kohlbecker zum ersten Preisträger bestimmt. Den zweiten Preis erhielt erneut Ungers, auf die folgenden Plätze kamen Arata Isozaki, Richard Rogers und Hans Kollhoff; Ulrike Lauber und Wolfram Wöhr bekamen einen Sonderpreis zugesprochen.

Piano/Kohlbecker haben sich streng an die Vorgaben gehalten; eine entscheidende Änderung war die Neusetzung des öffentlich-urbanen Schwerpunktes in die alte Potsdamer Straße mit einer neuen Piazza. Die kompakte

The design was played up in the architectural press. Yet the accusation that Rogers was acting purely in the interest of the property owners, who, moreover, had duped the Senate with their unsolicited counter-proposal, gave rise to an unexpected political alliance which brought about the rejection of the scheme. The Berlin architect Jürgen Sawade went so far as to call for his British colleague to be banned from the city.[18] Rogers spoke of the episode as the most awful experience of his life.[19] To avoid a loss of face, the Senate, which through its overly hasty sale of the Daimler property had precipitated the fiasco to begin with, had no choice but to stick to its decision. This one last time it was able to stand up to the all-powerful investors and, ironically, in so doing won the approval of the architectural associations. It exercised further influence through its strict design guidelines for Leipziger Platz.

In the following months Hilmer & Sattler's urban design concept underwent a number of changes en route to its adoption as the basis for the architectural design competition for the Daimler-Benz property.[20] One demand placed on the entrants was to plan the development as a connecting member between the Kulturforum and Potsdamer Platz. The cornice height was set at 35 metres, the overall building height limited to two additional set-back storeys. At Potsdamer Platz and at the Landwehrkanal a building height of 80 metres was allowed. A street tunnel would be considered in order to facilitate traffic connections and provide utility access. Fourteen architects were invited to participate. On 4 September, 1992, the team of Renzo Piano and Christoph Kohlbecker was awarded first prize in the competition. Ungers again took second place, followed by Arata Isozaki, Richard Rogers and Hans Kollhoff, while a special prize was awarded to Ulrike Lauber and Wolfram Wöhr.

Piano and Kohlbecker adhered strictly to the competition design requirements. They made a decisive change, however, in removing the

Lageplan des 1. Preises von
Renzo Piano und Christoph
Kohlbecker im
Realisierungswettbewerb
des Daimler-Benz Areals
am Potsdamer Platz,
September 1992.

Site plan, first-place entry
by Renzo Piano and
Christoph Kohlbecker in
the architectural design
competition for the
Daimler-Benz property at
Potsdamer Platz, Septem-
ber 1992.

Blockstruktur an der Straße geht über in eine
freistehende Bebauung, deren Form und Volu-
men sich an den Bauten Scharouns orientie-
ren. In diesen Bauten sollen ein Musicaltheater, ein Ausstellungspavillon und die Erweiterung der Bibliothek Platz finden und so die
„Kultur-Piazza" umfangen. Die Piazza ist teilweise von Wasserflächen durchbrochen, leitet
formal vom „Festland" zu den frei schwim-
menden Bauten des Kulturforums über; geplant ist ein Durchgang in das Foyer der
Staatsbibliothek. Am Potsdamer Platz und am
Landwehrkanal akzentuieren höhere Bauteile
die Anlage.

Bis zum Frühjahr 1993 wurde der Plan überar-
beitet: an der zentralen Piazza fokussiert sich
das öffentlich-kulturelle Leben, für die Biblio-
thekserweiterung war nun die Spielbank vorgesehen. Die neue Eichhornstraße teilt das
Quartier nun in drei Bereiche und bildet eine
weitere Querverbindung zur Piazza. Die Gebäudehöhe reduzierten Piano/Kohlbecker auf
28 Meter im inneren Bereich, nur an der neuen
Potsdamer Straße sind die Gebäude 35 Meter
hoch. Bei der debis-Zentrale am Landwehrkanal wird die Blockstruktur zu einem Bauteil zusammengefaßt, im Inneren liegt ein großer
Ausstellungsraum. Vom *Weinhaus Huth* erstreckt sich nach Süden eine überdachte Passage. Im April 1993 wurde dieser Masterplan
der Öffentlichkeit präsentiert.

public focus of the development from the
Potsdamer Platz itself to the old Potsdamer
Strasse, where they placed a new piazza.
Here, the compact block structure of the
street gave way to free-standing buildings
whose forms and volumes pointedly echoed
Hans Scharoun's neighbouring works. A musical theatre, an exhibition pavilion and the
extension of the Staatsbibliothek were to be
accommodated here, enclosing the "cultural
piazza" on its west side. The piazza is partially broken up by water elements indicat-
ing the transition from the "mainland' to the
free-floating structures of the Kulturforum.
A connecting passage leading into the foyer
of the Staatsbibliothek is planned. The opposite ends of the development are accentu-
ated by high-rise towers at Potsdamer Platz
and at the Landwehrkanal.

The plan was reworked until early 1993. The
central piazza became the focus of public
and cultural activities, while a casino took
the place of the library expansion. The new
Eichhornstrasse divided the area into three
sections and provided a further cross-con-
nection to the piazza. Piano and Kohlbecker
reduced the cornice height in the inner area
to 28 metres, maintaining it at 35 metres
only in the new Potsdamer Strasse. The block
structure housing the debis headquarters at
the Landwehrkanal was drawn together into
a single building volume containing a large
exhibition space. A covered mall stretched
from *Weinhaus Huth* southwards. In April
1993 the masterplan was presented to the
public. By agreement of the Senate, which
now, with the district of Tiergarten and the
investor, debis (a daughter company of Daimler-Benz founded 1 January, 1993), trans-
ferred management of the project to the municipal building administration, the masterplan was made the framework for the planning of the individual properties. As stated
in the competition announcement, responsi-
bility for the general planning was awarded
to Piano/Kohlbecker. The design of the development's 19 individual buildings went to

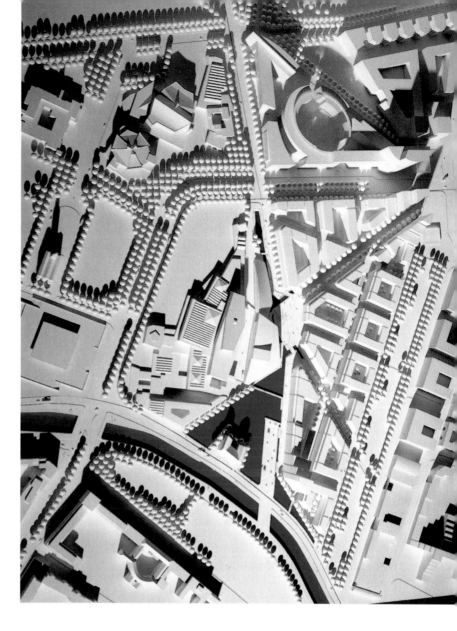

In Abstimmung mit dem Senat, der jetzt die Verantwortung der Bauverwaltung übertrug, mit dem Bezirk Tiergarten und dem Investor, der Projektgesellschaft debis (einer am 1. Januar 1993 gegründeten Tochtergesellschaft von Daimler-Benz), diente er als Rahmen für die Einzelplanungen. Wie bereits in der Auslobung beschrieben, erhielten Piano/Kohlbecker die Gesamtplanung, die weiteren Preisträger bzw. Teilnehmer Kollhoff, Moneo, Isozaki, Rogers, Lauber/Wöhr und Ungers, der jedoch nach anfänglicher Mitarbeit zurücktrat, wurden mit der Planung für die insgesamt 19 Bauten beauftragt.

Der letzte Schritt schließlich war der im Juni 1994 fertiggestellte Realisierungsplan, dem schon im März der Berliner Senat und die Abgeordneten zugestimmt hatten; bereits am 11. Oktober 1993 war symbolisch der erste Spatenstich vollzogen worden. Die rund 340.000 m² Bruttogeschoßfläche verteilen sich auf 56% Büro, 19% Wohnen, 11% Einzelhandel, 9% Hotel und 5% Kultur. Aufgrund des mittlerweile fest geplanten Autotunnels konnte nicht nur der oberirdische Verkehr entzerrt werden, sondern es bot sich auch die Gelegenheit, durch weitere Untergeschosse Raum zu gewinnen. So wurde die Passage zur Shopping Mall mit einer zusätzlichen unterirdischen Ebene geformt.

Parallel zu dem Wettbewerb für das Daimler-Gelände schrieb auch Sony im Mai 1992 eine Konkurrenz unter sieben geladenen Architekten aus, die bereits im August zugunsten des deutsch-amerikanischen Architekten Helmut Jahn entschieden wurde; William Pedersen und Walter A. Noebel belegten die folgenden Plätze, Meinhard von Gerkans und Herman Hertzbergers Entwürfe wurden angekauft.[21] Gefordert war, auf der Grundlage des offiziellen Masterplans, vor allem eine architektonische Gestalt von besonderem künstlerischen Gewicht, mit identitätsstiftender Form sowohl für die Stadt wie für das Unternehmen zu schaffen. Im Inneren des 26.000 m² großen Areals soll eine überdachte, öffentlich zugängliche Piazza untergebracht werden, die

further prize-winners or participants in the competition, including Kollhoff, Moneo, Isozaki, Rogers, and Lauber/Wöhr. Ungers was also initially engaged but soon stepped down.

The building plan marked the final step. This was finished in June 1994, after approval by the municipal administration and city council in March. The groundbreaking had been held on 11 October, 1993. The total of 340,000 square metres of floor space included 56% for offices, 19% for residential use, 11% for retail, 9% for hotel, and 5% for cultural uses. Planning for the automobile tunnel had by now been finalised, allowing not just a reduction in street-level traffic,

Modellaufnahme der überarbeiteten Fassung des Masterplans von Renzo Piano und Christoph Kohlbecker für das Daimler-Benz-Areal am Potsdamer Platz, April 1992.

Model, revised version of masterplan by Renzo Piano and Christoph Kohlbecker for the Daimler-Benz property at Potsdamer Platz, April 1992.

dem Vorwurf begegnet, daß nicht der öffentliche Raum privatisiert, sondern der geschlossene Raum geöffnet wird. Jahn entwarf ein Ensemble mit einheitlich gestalteten Glasfassaden, das sich aus mehreren Bauteilen zusammensetzt. Als spektakuläre Blickpunkte bieten sich das Hochhaus am Potsdamer Platz und die technizistische Dachkonstruktion über dem Forum dar. Von dem alten *Hotel Esplanade* soll nur die Fassade als historisches Relikt erhalten bleiben.

Es erging die Empfehlung an Jahn, die ausgreifende Kante am Kemperplatz zurückzunehmen und die Bauflucht der Bellevuestraße zu respektieren, die Größe und Terrassengliederung der Piazza zu überprüfen und insgesamt bei der architektonischen Gestaltung größtmögliche Zurückhaltung und Klarheit im Sinne der Berliner Tradition anzustreben. Dem Auslober wurde nahegelegt, andere Architekten für die Realisierung mit einzubeziehen. Der publizistische Wirbel um die Gestaltung am Potsdamer Platz hatte sich beruhigt, dennoch fiel die Wertung negativ aus: Die eingeladenen Architekten entsprächen der Wunschliste der amerikanischen Kommerzarchitektur, der Entwurf von Jahn sei ein typisches Investorenprojekt, introvertiert und nach außen

but the addition of underground floors as well, specifically a further subterranean level in the pedestrian passage to the shopping mall.

In May 1992, parallel to the competition for the Daimler-Benz site, Sony invited seven selected architects to submit design schemes for its adjacent property. The following August, German-American Helmut Jahn was named the winner. William Pedersen and Walter A. Noebel took second and third places, respectively, and submissions by Meinhard von Gerkan and Herman Hertzberger were also purchased.[21] On the basis of the official masterplan, Sony called for, above all, an architectural composition of high artistic merit, one that would contribute to both Berlin's urban and Sony's corporate identity. The interior of the 26,000-square-metre site was to contain a covered, publicly accessible piazza, to head off potential criticism that the development constituted the privatisation of public space. Jahn designed an ensemble of several blocks clad in uniform glass facades. A high-rise tower at Potsdamer Platz and a technically elaborate roof construction over the inner forum comprised the spectacular visual focal points of the project. Of the old *Hotel Esplanade,* only the facade was to be maintained and integrated in the development, due to its value as historic relic.

Jahn was requested to pull back the overhanging building edge at Kemperplatz in deference to the Bellevuestrasse property line, and to revise the piazza's proportions and terrace relationships. He was generally urged to strive for a maximum of reserve and architectural design clarity in accordance with Berlin tradition. The Senate was advised to also engage other architects in the project's realisation. Though the press flurry over the design efforts at Potsdamer Platz had subsided, the initial response to the Sony plans was negative. Critics complained that the roster of invited architects read like an American corporate wish list, and that

Modellaufnahme des 1. Preises von Helmut Jahn im Realisierungswettbewerb des Sony-Geländes am Potsdamer Platz, August 1992.

Model, first-place entry by Helmut Jahn in the architectural design competition for the Sony property at Potsdamer Platz, April 1992.

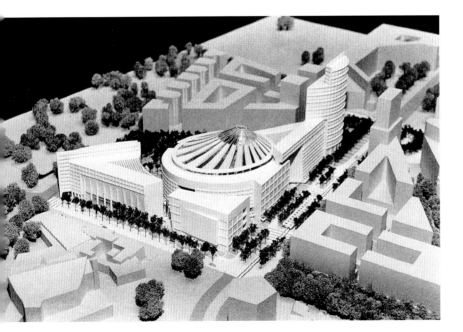

protzig. Zudem hätten die städtebaulichen Vorgaben kaum Beachtung gefunden, das Hochhaus sei um 17 Meter höher und die geforderte Nutzungsmischung schlicht unterlaufen worden.[22]

Vollkommen unspektakulär fiel schließlich die Entscheidung des Investors Asea Brown Boveri/ABB für sein Baugebiet östlich des alten Bahnhofsgeländes aus. Nach einem internationalen Wettbewerb unter acht geladenen Architekten fiel im Juni 1993 die Wahl auf Giorgio Grassi.[23] Er lehnte sich sehr eng an den Hilmer & Sattler-Entwurf an und unterteilte das rechteckige Grundstück in vier H- bzw. U-förmige Blöcke, die er als „Palasttypus" beschreibt. Der Kopfbau am Potsdamer Platz zitiert mit seiner Rundung das einst an diesem Ort stehende *Haus Vaterland*. Wie auf dem Daimler-Benz-Grundstück werden auch die weiteren Preisträger, Diener & Diener, Jürgen Sawade und Peter Schweger, mit der Ausführung betraut.

Die Planungen am Lenné-Dreieck wurden stark von den sich verzögernden Tiefbauarbeiten für den Regionalbahnhof und die Tunnelanlagen beeinflußt. Nach dem städtebaulichen Bild von Hilmer & Sattler, die an der Nordgrenze mit sieben 10geschossigen Stadtvillen den Übergang zum Tiergarten bilden, ist bis zum Jahr 2000 nur ein Bürohaus fertiggestellt worden. In Planung ist das letzte Hochhaus an der Ebertstraße, das Kollhoff für ein Bankhaus errichten wird. Die weiteren Planungen und Nutzungen stehen zur Zeit noch nicht fest. Ähnliches gilt für die Bauten des Leipziger Platzes, wo teilweise ungeklärte Grundstücksverhältnisse, aber auch komplizierter Baugrund wegen des Verlaufs der U-Bahntrasse eine Realisierung verhindern. Für einen Großteil der Grundstücke liegen bereits seit 1998 prämierte Wettbewerbsentwürfe vor. Die Bebauungspläne wurden 1995 festgelegt und sehen eine Traufhöhe von 22,5 Metern vor; ein Gebäudekranz, in dem ausschließlich Wohnungen untergebracht werden dürfen, kann nach einem Rücksprung um zwei Meter 35 Meter erreichen. Eine Gestaltungsvorgabe besagt, daß kein ver-

Jahn's scheme was typical corporate architecture – a distasteful combination of introversion and outward swagger. They accused the architect of disregarding the stated planning guidelines in designing the tower at Potsdamer Platz 17 metres higher than permitted and circumventing the required functional mix of the development.[22]

In contrast to Sony, property owner Asea Brown Boveri/ABB opted for the unspectacular. From the eight architects invited to enter the international design competition for its property to the east of the former railway station site, the corporation selected Giorgio Grassi in June 1993.[23] He held very closely to the underlying Hilmer & Sattler urban design concept, placing on the long rectangular site four H- or U-shaped buildings. The head of this row of "palace type" blocks, the rounded building at Potsdamer Platz, deliberately recalls the *Haus Vaterland,* the famous historic occupant of the site. As in the Daimler-Benz development, the competition's further prize-winners – in this case Diener & Diener, Jürgen Sawade and Peter Schweger – were entrusted with the execution of the individual buildings.

The development of Lenné-Dreieck has been slowed considerably by construction delays on the regional railway station and its approach tunnels. Hilmer & Sattler's urban design concept calls for seven ten-storey urban villas along the north border of the site to provide a transition to the Tiergarten. Just one office building has been completed as of the year 2000. The last high-rise in Ebertstrasse, a bank building by Kollhoff, is in the planning stage. The further uses of the area have yet to be determined and the building plans finalised. Leipziger Platz hangs in a similar state of limbo, its realisation hindered by unresolved questions of property ownership and complications in site preparation due to the underground train line that passes beneath it. For many of the properties at Leipziger Platz winning competition designs have awaited action since 1998. The

Modell des ABB-Geländes.

Model of the ABB property.

construction guidelines were set in 1995 and call for a streetfront building height of 22.5 metres. Above this, additional storeys exclusively for residential use may rise at a two-metre set-back to a total height of 35 metres. A design requirement states that no reflective glass, and only light-coloured, natural materials may be used.

The last competition for Potsdamer Platz, held in 1995, was for the design of two green areas, one on the west part of the Lenné-Dreieck and the other on the site of the former Potsdamer railway station. It was announced internationally and open to both architects and landscape architects. From the 154 concepts presented, second prizes were awarded to two schemes. Their authors, the Dutch office of Maike van Stiphout and Bruno Doedens and the Swiss landscape architects Toni Weber and Lucius Saurer, were called on to rework their designs.[24] In November of that year the Dutch firm received the contract, though work on the project will not commence until building construction has been completed on the site, probably in 2001. Another nearby undertaking, the landscaping of the area around Gleisdreieck, deserves note as an important contribution to Berlin's environmental quality. Until early 2000 the site was the location of the building logistics control centre for the work at Potsdamer Platz. The project is being financed in part by the Potsdamer Platz investors, as compensation for the loss of green space through the construction of the quarter.[25]

All's well that end's well? Not so fast. The latest, though likely not last critique levelled at the developments at Potsdamer Platz went largely unnoticed in the commotion surrounding debis' opening ceremony on 3 October, 1998: Berlin's Cardinal Sterzinsky lamented the lack of a space for church activities.

spiegeltes Glas, sondern nur die Verwendung von hellen, natürlichen Materialien erlaubt ist. 1995 wurde der letzte, diesmal landschaftsplanerische Realisierungswettbewerb für den Potsdamer Platz durchgeführt, der international ausgeschrieben war und Architekten wie Landschaftsarchitekten offen stand. Er hatte die Gestaltung von zwei Grünzügen zum Inhalt, die auf dem westlichen Teil des Lenné-Dreiecks und auf dem Gelände des ehemaligen Potsdamer Bahnhofs angelegt werden sollten. Von den 154 eingereichten Arbeiten wurden die Entwürfe des holländischen Büros Maike van Stiphout und Bruno Doedens sowie die Schweizer Gartenarchitekten Toni Weber und Lucius Saurer jeweils mit einem zweiten Preis ausgewählt und zur Überarbeitung aufgefordert.[24] Das niederländische Büro erhielt schließlich im November den Zuschlag für die Ausführung, die aber erst nach den Baumaßnahmen, voraussichtlich ab 2001, umgesetzt werden. Als wichtiger ökologischer Beitrag ist die Begrünung des bis Anfang 2000 von der Baulogistik genutzten Geländes um das Gleisdreieck anzusehen, das als Ausgleich der bebauten Fläche am Potsdamer Platz teilweise von den Investoren finanziert wird.[25]

Ende gut, alles gut? Mitnichten: Eine vorläufig letzte Kritik an den Planungen verhallte im Trubel der bevorstehenden Eröffnung des debis-Geländes am 3. Oktober 1998: Der Berliner Kardinal Sterzinsky beklagte das Fehlen eines Raumes für kirchliche Aktivitäten.

1 Gerwin Zohlen, Erblast des Mythos. Das Verfahren Potsdamer/Leipziger Platz, in: Ein Stück Großstadt als Experiment, Planungen am Potsdamer Platz in Berlin (Katalog des Deutschen Architektur Museums Frankfurt a.M.), Vittorio M. Lampugnani, Romana Schneider (Hg.), Stuttgart 1994, S. 14 ff.

2 in: Berlin – Denkmal oder Denkmodell?, Kristin Feireiss (Hg.), Berlin 1988, S. 58 ff.

3 Dieter Hoffmann-Axthelm, Die Stadt, das Geld und die Demokratie, in: Arch+, Nr. 105/106, Oktober 1990, S. 107 ff.

4 Berlin Morgen, Ideen für das Herz einer Großstadt, Vittorio M. Lampugnani, Michael Mönninger (Hg.), Stuttgart 1991.

5 Bruno Flierl, Hoch hinaus? Zum Medienspektakel „Berlin Morgen", in: Stadtbauwelt 109 (=Bauwelt 1991, H. 12), S. 614 f.

6 otl aicher, berlin wird hauptstadt, in: Arch+, Nr. 108, August 1991, S. 20 ff.

7 Werner Sewing, Berlinische Architektur, in: Arch+, Nr. 122, Juni 1994, S. 64.

8 Interview mit J. P. Kleihues, in: archithese 1992, H. 2, S. 25 f.

9 Gruppe 9. Dezember, Charta für die Mitte von Berlin, in: Stadtbauwelt 109 (=Bauwelt 1991, H. 12), S. 562 ff.

10 Gerwin Zohlen, in: Süddeutsche Zeitung, 21.9.1993.

11 Bernhard Schneider, Das Stadtforum Berlin – Ein politisches Instrument eigener Art, in: archithese 1992, H. 2, S. 38 ff.

12 AIV Ideenkonkurrenz Potsdamer Platz / Leipziger Platz, Dokumentation, o.O., o.J. (Berlin 1992)

13 Potsdamer und Leipziger Platz / Internationaler engerer Wettbewerb/Ausschreibung, Senatsverwaltung für Stadtentwicklung und Umweltschutz (Hg.), Berlin 1991, S. 25 ff.

14 Städtebaulicher Wettbewerb Potsdamer/Leipziger Platz, Ergebnisprotokoll, Senatsverwaltung für Stadtentwicklung und Umweltschutz (Hg.), Berlin 1991

15 Rem Koolhaas, Berlin: The massacre of ideas, in: Frankfurter Allgemeine Zeitung, 16.10.1991

16 Frankfurter Allgemeine Zeitung, 16.10.1991

17 Der Tagesspiegel, 22.10.1991

18 Der Tagesspiegel, 26.10.1991

19 Interview mit Richard Rogers, in: Lettre International, Frühjahr 1993, S. 77.

20 Potsdamer Platz Realisierungswettbewerb, Auslobung, Daimler-Benz AG (Hg.), Berlin 1992. Die Ergebnisse sind dokumentiert in: Ein Stück Großstadt als Experiment, Planungen am Potsdamer Platz in Berlin, s. Anm. 1, S. 86 ff.

21 Architektenwettbewerb Potsdamer Platz, Sony Berlin (Hg.), Berlin 1992.

22 Falk Jaeger, in: Der Tagesspiegel, 19.8.1992

23 Sebastian Redecke, Potsdamer Platz, Teil 3, in: Bauwelt 1993, H. 26, S. 1412, 1415 ff.

24 2 Parks am Potsdamer Platz, Internationaler landschaftsplanerischer Realisierungs- und Ideenwettbewerb, Senatsverwaltung für Stadtentwicklung und Umweltschutz (Hg.), Berlin 1995

25 Margot Wieg, Bauleitplanung Potsdamer/Leipziger Platz, in: Bauwelt 1994, H. 36, S. 1998 ff.

1 Gerwin Zohlen, Erblast des Mythos. Das Verfahren Potsdamer / Leipziger Platz, in: Ein Stück Großstadt als Experiment, Planungen am Potsdamer Platz in Berlin (Catalogue of the Deutsches Architektur Museum Frankfurt a.M.), Vittorio M. Lampugnani, Romana Schneider (eds.), Stuttgart 1994, pp. 14 seq.

2 in: Berlin – Denkmal oder Denkmodell?, Kristin Feireiss (ed.), Berlin 1988, pp. 58 seq.

3 Dieter Hoffmann-Axthelm, Die Stadt, das Geld und die Demokratie, in: Arch+, nos. 105/106, October 1990, pp. 107 seq.

4 Berlin Morgen, Ideen für das Herz einer Großstadt, Vittorio M. Lampugnani, Michael Mönninger (eds.), Stuttgart 1991.

5 Bruno Flierl, Hoch hinaus? Zum Medienspektakel "Berlin Morgen", in: Stadtbauwelt 109 (=Bauwelt 1991, no. 12), pp. 614 seq.

6 otl aicher, berlin wird hauptstadt, in: Arch+, no. 108, August 1991, pp. 20 seq.

7 Werner Sewing, Berlinische Architektur, in: Arch+, no. 122, June 1994, p. 64.

8 Interview with J. P. Kleihues, in: archithese 1992, no. 2, pp. 25-26.

9 Gruppe 9. Dezember, Charta für die Mitte von Berlin, in: Stadtbauwelt 109 (=Bauwelt 1991, no. 12), pp. 562 seq.

10 Gerwin Zohlen, in: Süddeutsche Zeitung, 21 Sept.,1993.

11 Bernhard Schneider, Das Stadtforum Berlin – Ein politisches Instrument eigener Art, in: archithese 1992, no. 2, pp. 38 seq.

12 AIV Ideenkonkurrenz Potsdamer Platz / Leipziger Platz, documentation, s.l., s.a. (Berlin 1992)

13 Potsdamer und Leipziger Platz / Internationaler engerer Wettbewerb / Ausschreibung, Senatsverwaltung für Stadtentwicklung und Umweltschutz (ed.), Berlin 1991, pp. 25 seq.

14 Städtebaulicher Wettbewerb Potsdamer/Leipziger Platz, Ergebnisprotokoll, Senatsverwaltung für Stadtentwicklung und Umweltschutz (ed.), Berlin 1991

15 Rem Koolhaas, Berlin: The massacre of ideas, in: Frankfurter Allgemeine Zeitung, 16 Oct., 1991

16 Frankfurter Allgemeine Zeitung, 16 Oct., 1991

17 Der Tagesspiegel, 22 Oct., 1991

18 Der Tagesspiegel, 26 Oct., 1991

19 Interview with Richard Rogers, in: Lettre International, spring 1993, p. 77.

20 Potsdamer Platz Realisierungswettbewerb, Auslobung, Daimler-Benz AG (ed.), Berlin 1992. The results are documented in: Ein Stück Großstadt als Experiment, Planungen am Potsdamer Platz in Berlin, see note 1, pp. 86 seq.

21 Architektenwettbewerb Potsdamer Platz, Sony Berlin (ed.), Berlin 1992.

22 Falk Jaeger, in: Der Tagesspiegel, 19 Aug., 1992

23 Sebastian Redecke, Potsdamer Platz, Teil 3, in: Bauwelt 1993, no. 26, pp. 1412, 1415 seq.

24 2 Parks am Potsdamer Platz, Internationaler landschaftsplanerischer Realisierungs- und Ideenwettbewerb, Senatsverwaltung für Stadtentwicklung und Umweltschutz (ed.), Berlin 1995

25 Margot Wieg, Bauleitplanung Potsdamer/Leipziger Platz, in: Bauwelt 1994, no. 36, pp. 1998 seq.

Werner Sewing

Herz, Kunstherz oder Themenpark?

Deutungsversuche des Phänomens Potsdamer Platz

Spätestens seit dem Umzug der Regierung und des Parlaments von Bonn nach Berlin im Sommer 1999 hat sich nun endlich auch der Triumph Berlins als Touristenmetropole Deutschlands und Europas eingestellt. Die neue Mitte der deutschen Hauptstadt ist nach Jahren beharrlicher Stadtwerbung – man denke an die Baustellen als Schaustellen – als räumlicher Kristallisationspunkt eines neuen Nationalstolzes („Mal schauen, wo meine Steuergelder geblieben sind") und als Projektionsfläche für Weltstadtsehnsüchte angenommen. Es versteht sich, daß es zunächst nicht um das reale Berlin (welches von den vielen?) geht, sondern um Bilder, *images* und ihre Inszenierung. Der Potsdamer Platz ist neben dem Reichstag mit seiner Hauptattraktion, der Kuppel, und dem Brandenburger Tor vielleicht das zentrale städtische Ereignis im Boom der neuen Mitte: „Touris Liebling", wie es in einer Werbeseite einer Berliner Zeitung kurz und griffig hieß. Als pulsierendes Herz der Stadt, als das jahrzehntelang schmerzlich vermißte Zentrum der zerrissenen Metropole wird die aus der nur noch von den Geistern der Geschichte bewohnten „Wüste", so Renzo Piano, von Mauer, Todesstreifen und Brachland erstandene Retortenstadt in der Lokalpresse begrüßt. Diese Deutung verdichtet sich gegenwärtig zur Folklore, selbstverständlich ist sie dennoch nicht. Die Wettbewerbe Anfang der 90er Jahre, die auch den Leipziger Platz umfaßten, hatten eine sehr weiträumige Bestimmung des Platzes lanciert. Nehmen wir dieses Gebiet als Ganzes, so ist es für eine Bestandsaufnahme sicher noch zu früh. Von den vier Teilgebieten ist das nördliche Tortenstück, das Lenné-Dreieck, erst mit einem kleineren Gebäude besetzt. Östlich des

Heart, Artificial Heart, or Theme Park?

Trying to make sense of Potsdamer Platz

The move of the government and parliament from Bonn to Berlin in summer 1999 can be seen to mark Berlin's triumph not only as the nation's political centre, but also as the tourist capital of Germany and Europe. After years of persistent self-promotion – the construction site as tourist sight – Berlin is now recognised as the spatial crystallisation point of a new-found national pride ("let's have a look what's become of my tax money"). It has also assumed the role of projection surface for Germans' big-city ambitions and desires. Needless to say, this upwelling of spirit is more directly concerned with the production of images than with the real Berlin.

Alongside the Reichstag, newly crowned with its glass dome, and the Brandenburg Gate, Potsdamer Platz ranks as perhaps the central urban event in the boom of Berlin's new Mitte – "tourist's favourite," as dubbed in a fullpage Berlin newspaper advertisement. The local press has hailed the quarter's development as the revival of the pulsating heart of the city. Rising from the "desert," in Renzo Piano's words, the barren no-man's-land where for decades only the ghosts of history dwelled, the test-tube city has claimed its place as the painfully missed centre of the sundered metropolis. This sentiment is rapidly solidifying as legend, historical reality notwithstanding. The design competitions for Potsdamer Platz in the early nineties staked out a wide area that included Leipziger Platz. Taken as a whole, it's certainly too early to make a full assessment of the results. Only one small building presently stands on the Lenné-Dreieck, the small, wedge-shaped, northernmost section of the development area, and

alten Bahngeländes des Potsdamer Bahnhofs, das demnächst als Tilla-Durieux-Park neu entstehen soll, ist das Projekt Park Kolonnaden noch im Bau. Abgesehen von dem Eckbau an der Stresemannstraße, der mit seiner runden Ecke entfernt an das legendäre *Haus Vaterland*, dessen Standort er nun beerbt, erinnern soll, werden die Kolonnaden aber nur Büros und einige Appartements aufnehmen. Auch der Leipziger Platz, dessen achteckige barocke Grundrißfigur man nun langsam mit neun- bis elfgeschossigen Gebäuden im bekannten rationalistischen Stil des neuen Berlin wieder aufzufüllen beginnt, wird immer noch von der temporären Info Box beherrscht, die seit 1995 die Attraktion des Baustellentourismus war, deren Tage, trotz ungebrochener Besuchernachfrage, nun aber gezählt scheinen.

Der Potsdamer Platz: an ihn erinnerten nach dem Krieg und vor allem nach der Abrißwut der Nachkriegszeit außer wenigen Straßenverläufen, etwa einem baumbestandenen Stück der alten Potsdamer Straße, nur noch ein Rest des wilhelminischen Nobelhotels *Esplanade* an der Bellevuestraße und das sogar noch bewohnte *Haus Huth* zwischen Potsdamer und Linkstraße. Das *Esplanade* wurde inzwischen kunstvoll tranchiert und mit seinen opulenten Festsälen in das Sony Center integriert. Das *Haus Huth*, vorbildlich restauriert, bietet, allerdings eingezwängt zwischen Großblöcken nun der Alten Potsdamer Straße den einzigen bauhistorischen Halt.

Außer dem Mythos, der gewissermaßen als symbolische Anschubfinanzierung der urbanen Herztransplantation dient, besteht der Potsdamer Platz nun vor allem aus dem bereits im Herbst 1998 nach fünf Jahren Bauzeit teilweise eröffnete debis-Areal, mit vier Milliarden das ehrgeizigste Projekt im hauptstädtischen Wiederaufbau, zeitlich, mit zwei Milliarden Investitionssumme aber auch in der Dimension, gefolgt vom Sony Center, das nach einem provisorischen Start im Januar erst im Juni 2000 sein „Grand Opening" feierte.

Beide Projekte – und ihre auf den ersten Blick sehr konträren Stadtvisionen – repräsentieren

the site of the old Potsdamer railway station is awaiting development as Tilla Durieux Park. Just to the east of the former station, the Park Kolonnaden are still under construction. With the exception of the corner building at Stresemannstrasse, which vaguely recalls the legendary *Haus Vaterland*, whose site it inherits, the Kolonnaden will house only offices and a few apartments. The octagonal baroque ground plan of Leipziger Platz is slowly beginning to fill up with nine- to eleven-storey buildings in the familiar rationalistic style of the new Berlin. It is, however, still dominated by the temporary Info Box, which since 1995 has been the central attraction of the city's building site tourism but whose days now appear numbered, despite the unabated stream of visitors.

World War II and, especially, the post-war frenzy of the wrecking ball left little to remember Potsdamer Platz by. Beyond a few razed streetscapes, among them a stretch of the old Potsdamer Strasse with a number of determined trees still clinging to it, all that remained was the Wilhelminian ruin of the luxurious *Hotel Esplanade* in Bellevuestrasse and the still-inhabited *Haus Huth* between Potsdamer and Linkstrasse. The *Esplanade* has been artfully carved up and, with its opulent banquet halls, incorporated in the new Sony Center. The *Haus Huth* has undergone an exemplary restoration and now, though sandwiched between the large neighbouring blocks, provides the Alte Potsdamer Strasse with its only substantial historical anchor.

Apart from the myth, which in a sense serves as symbolic start-up financing for the urban heart transplant, Potsdamer Platz at present consists of two main sections. The debis development, partially opened in autumn 1998 after five years' construction, constitutes an investment of four billion D-marks, making it the most ambitious project in the rebuilding of the capital. This is followed chronologically and financially by the two-billion-mark Sony Center, which, after a provisional start in January 2000, held its grand opening in June.

bereits jetzt die urbanen Potentiale des Stadt-quartiers. Was auf dem Höhepunkt der Wett-bewerbskontroversen bis ca. 1993 als Gegen-satz von „europäischer" und „amerikanischer" Stadt stilisiert worden war, hat nun Gestalt an-genommen und füllt sich mit Leben.

Während der Bauzeit war die Architekturdis-kussion verstummt. Die Sympathien und Hoff-nungen galten nun bei aller Skepsis dem Pro-jekt von debis, dessen Masterplaner Renzo Pia-no aus Genua am ehesten zugetraut wurde, den Spagat zwischen gediegener moderner Ar-chitektur und den Konventionen des traditio-nellen Städtebaus zu schaffen. Anders als in der Friedrichstadt sollte am Potsdamer Platz keine rückwärtsgewandte Kulisse mit preußi-scher Anmutung entstehen. Das Sony-Projekt hingegen ließ eine wenig stadtverträgliche Selbstdarstellung des globalen Konzerns und seines Architekten Helmut Jahn erwarten. Feuilleton und Fachpresse warteten und hiel-ten sich bedeckt.

Nun wurden aber die Stadtmanager aktiv. Auf deren Bühne wurde die neugierige Öffentlich-keit von rührigen Event-Regisseuren mit der Erotik der Baustellen auf die kommende neue Mitte eingestimmt. Auch diese versprach ein Event zu werden.

Anfang Oktober 1998 berichtete *Le Monde* in einem zweiseitigen Artikel mit einer Schlag-zeile auf dem Titelblatt über *La revolution de Berlin*. Was konnte – immerhin neun Jahre nach dem Fall der Mauer, der am ehesten als Revolu-tion hätte bezeichnet werden können – einen solchen Titel rechtfertigen? Tatsächlich wurde auch nicht von einem Sturm auf die Bastille, sondern von der Einweihung einer Bastille be-richtet: von der Eröffnung einer modernen Fe-stung des Konsums, sogar durch den deutschen Bundespräsidenten höchstpersönlich. Was da-mals oft noch respektlos als „Daimler City" be-zeichnet wurde, ist heute längst „Der Potsda-mer Platz". Indem wir bereits jetzt den Teil für das Ganze nehmen, bestätigen wir die gelun-gene Definition dieses Stadtteils durch debis. Nach den Hunderttausenden von Besuchern al-lein in den ersten Wochen nach der Eröffnung

These two projects – and their seemingly con-trary urban visions – at this stage represent the urban potentials of this quarter. Con-trastingly branded as "European" and "Amer-ican" urban form at the height of the compe-tition controversies up to around 1993, the plans have taken on concrete shape and are filling with life.

During the construction period the architec-tural debate fell silent. Despite strong scep-ticism, sympathies and hopes sided mostly with the debis project, whose masterplanner, the Genoan Renzo Piano, was the architect most trusted to pull off the balancing act be-tween tasteful modern architecture and the conventions of traditional urban design. This project, unlike those of the Friedrichstadt, did not call for urban scenery in retrogressive Prussian guise. The Helmut Jahn-designed Sony project, on the other hand, generated pessimistic expectations for a show of cor-porate and architectural egotism. Keeping a low profile, the newspapers and architectural press waited. Meanwhile, the city authorities became active. Event directors took the stage and, with the erotic magnetism of the con-struction site, worked up enthusiasm among a curious public for the coming *neue Mitte*. This, too, promised to become an event.

At the beginning of October 1998 *Le Monde* published a two-page article on *La revolution de Berlin*. Was there anything to justify such a title nine years after the fall of the Wall, the event that more than any other might actually have been described as a revolution? In fact, the paper wasn't reporting on a storming of the Bastille, but rather the open-ing of one – of a modern fortress of con-sumption, by none other than the German Federal President. What was often snidely re-ferred to at that time as "Daimler City" has by now established itself as "Potsdamer Platz". In taking the part already standing for the as yet unfinished whole, we reaffirm debis' lead in defining the quarter. The storm of hundreds of thousands of visitors to the development during the first weeks after the

Blick auf das Sony-Areal.
Links: die Torsituation zur
Alten Potsdamer Straße.

View of the Sony development. On the left: the gate
configuration to the Alte
Potsdamer Straße.

ist der Sturm zwar abgeebbt, hat sich aber verstetigt. Die Betreiber sprechen seit Ende 1998 konstant von statistisch 70 000 Besuchern pro Tag, davon allein 100 000 an den Wochenenden, vorwiegend Touristen. Wenn auch, außer an den überfüllten Samstagen, der Augenschein diese Zahlen nicht ganz deckt, so ist der Vermarktungserfolg offensichtlich.

An den realen Potsdamer Platz, lange Zeit ein Symbol der Teilung der Stadt, davor und nun wieder nur eine Straßenkreuzung mit Verkehrschaos, stößt der neue Stadtteil jedoch nur am Rand mit zwei schüchternen Hochhäusern zwischen 80 und 101 Metern Höhe von den Stararchitekten Renzo Piano und Hans Kollhoff. Ergänzt wird diese „Torsituation" zur Alten Potsdamer Straße durch eine zweite zur sechsspurigen Durchgangsstraße der neuen Potsdamer Straße. Dieses täglich von 40 000 Autos befahrene Nadelör zwischen Ost und West ist, ganz wie der historische Potsdamer Platz, vor allem dank fehlender Verkehrsplanung überlaufen, also urban?

Nördlich dieser Schneise antwortet Sony mit einem 103 Meter hohen gläsernen Turmhaus von Helmut Jahn auf das steinerne Kollhoff-Gebäude. Letzteres wurde erst während des Baus um zwei weitere Geschosse erhöht, um Sony nun auf immerhin 101 Metern Höhe Paroli bieten zu können. Den Besuchern des

opening has subsided considerably, levelling off at an average of around 70,000 per day since the end of 1998, according to the operators. At weekends the number is said to be 100,000, most of whom are tourists. Except on the overcowded Saturdays, firsthand observation doesn't quite bear out these numbers. Nevertheless, the marketing success is obvious.

The actual Potsdamer Platz, long a symbol of the city's division, has again become what it was before World War II, simply a hectic street crossing. The new debis development tentatively reaches to the edge of the plaza with two high-rises of 80 and 101 metres by the star architects Renzo Piano and Hans Kollhoff. This 'gate configuration' to the Alte Potsdamer Strasse is complemented by a second, similar tower arrangement at the head of the new Potsdamer Strasse. With forty thousand cars travelling daily through this needle's eye between East and West, the overburdened intersection is, just like the historic Potsdamer Platz, a victim of failed traffic planning. Urbane?

To the north of this thoroughfare, Sony countered the brick-clad Kollhoff building with a 103-metre-high glass tower of its own, designed by Helmut Jahn. Not wanting to be cast in Sony's figurative shadow, the Kollhoff

50

Panoramas auf der Aussichtsterrasse des Kollhoff-Baus kann dies nur recht sein: Der Blick auf Berlin ist atemberaubend.

Warum aber die Hochhäuser? Zum Bild der traditionellen europäischen Stadt gehören diese nicht. Obendrein spielt gerade der Kollhoff-Turm unverhohlen auf amerikanische Vorbilder aus den 30er Jahren an: Chicago oder New York als europäische Städte? Auch legt die Zusammenrottung der Türme an der Kreuzung die Vermutung nahe, hier solle eine *skyline* oder *downtown* zeichenhaft dargestellt werden. Dabei sind die Türme zu klein, um als Wolkenkratzer, und zu wenige, um als Manhattan durchzugehen: *Skyline en miniature*.

Es fehlt im Bild nicht nur an Höhe, sondern auch an Tiefe. So endet der Blick von der „Torsituation" in die neue Potsdamer Straße schon nach zwei Blöcken hinter den Türmen, das Kulturforum, Symbol des alten West-Berlin, gerät als rätselhafte, goldschimmernde Fata Morgana in den Blick – und es gewinnt durch den Kontrast zum kompakten Potsdamer Platz.

Tiefe hingegen stellt sich bei den seitwärtigen Eingängen in die beiden Areale ein. Sony saugt die Blicke in das theatralisch unter einem kühnen Zeltdach inszenierte Oval seiner Plaza. Der Sony-Komplex ist die monumentale Großform geworden, welche die Planer befürchtet hatten – nicht zuletzt, weil versäumt

team added two storeys to its building while construction was underway, bringing it to within two metres of the Sony tower's height. Visitors to the observation deck of the Kollhoff building won't have any complaints – the views of the city are outstanding.

But why the high-rises? They don't belong to the image of the traditional European city. The Kollhoff tower even makes explicit reference to American models from the nineteen thirties. Chicago or New York transplanted to Europe? The bunching of the towers at the plaza suggests an emblematic *skyline* or *downtown*. They are, however, too small to be skyscrapers and too few to make a Manhattan: *skyline en miniature*.

The picture lacks not only height, but also depth. The view through the "gate" into the new Potsdamer Strasse is terminated two blocks down the street, where the Kulturforum, symbol of the old West Berlin, floats into view like a curious, shimmering gold mirage – and gains in presence through its contrast to the compact Potsdamer Platz.

The depth of field increases at the side entrances to the two developments. Sony draws the eye into its elliptical central plaza, theatrically laid out under a bold tent-like roof structure. The Sony complex has taken shape as just the sort of monumental form the

51

wurde, die riesigen Fensterfronten zu rhythmisieren, zu gliedern, und damit zu richtigen Fassaden werden zu lassen. Wenige Fenstertypen, obendrein von anderen Jahn-Bauten bekannt, werden seriell verbaut.

Spannung dagegen erzeugt die gelungene Fassade des Filmhauses an der neuen Potsdamer Straße. Hier wird deutlich, das der monolithische Charakter des Komplexes bei näherer Betrachtung sich auflöst in einzelne Baukörper von sehr heterogener Qualität. Zwischen ihnen öffnen sich viele Zugänge über die gesamte Gebäudehöhe zum erstaunlich extrovertierten Innenhof. Das Ergebnis ist paradox. Obwohl Sony dem Ideal einer Unternehmensmonokultur viel mehr entspricht als debis, erweist sich sein Innenhof nicht als geschlossener, privatisierter Raum, sondern eher als fast öffentlicher Raum. Geringe Konsumangebote, etwas Gastronomie (ein *Hofbräuhaus* und *Alex*), Multiplex, Imax, natürlich die „geretteten" Festsäle des ehemaligen *Hotels Esplanade*, ansonsten wird eben nur das geboten, was ein Medienmulti zu bieten hat. Entertainment ja, aber nicht Konsum mit allen Registern. Gegenüber dem Bombardement mit Kaufreizen bei debis herrscht hier eine fast asketische Zurückhaltung. Raum, obendrein dem Berliner Klima preisgegebener Raum, als Selbstzweck, als Luxus.

Die kühle Ästhetik der zu monotonen Wände des Ovals aus Glas, Edelstahl und Aluminiumbänderungen enthält zwar eine Absage an historische Reminiszenzen, verkörpert aber gleichwohl eine verständliche futuristische Übersetzung des Mythos vom Potsdamer Platz aus den 20er Jahren in die Logik eines modernen Medienkonzerns: Schau, Rummel, Massenvergnügen, Kommerz: Hereinspaziert! Das gigantische Zeltdach, nachts als leuchtendes Signal weithin in der Stadt sichtbar, verspricht Urbanität im kommerziellen Konzentrat: Zirkus. Damit, ob beabsichtigt, ist nicht bekannt, erweist Sony, nein, eher Jahn auch den gegenüberliegenden Bauten Scharouns mit ihrer Zeltsymbolik seine Reverenz. Die Frage, ob dies gute Architektur sei, ist nicht wichtig. Auch an anderen europäischen Magneten des Massen-

city's planners feared – in part because the designers opted not to articulate the vast streetfront glass curtains, which thus fail as true facades. The complex employs only a few different window types borrowed from other Jahn buildings and spreads them monotonously over the surfaces of its blocks.

In contrast, the successful facade of the Filmhaus at the new Potsdamer Strasse manages to create a certain tension. Here, a closer view reveals that the monolithic character of the complex is broken down into individual buildings of very heterogeneous quality. Between these, many full-height passages open to the surprisingly extroverted inner court. The result is paradoxical. Although the Sony development reflects the ideal of corporate monoculture much more obviously than does that of debis, its inner plaza turns out to be not a closed, privatised space, but rather an almost public one. Limited consumer offerings, some bars and restaurants, multiplex and Imax cinemas, and of course the "rescued" banquet halls of the former *Hotel Esplanade* – otherwise, what is on offer here is exactly what you would expect from an international media conglomerate. Entertainment, yes, but not consumption across the full spectrum. As opposed to the commercial bombardment at debis, an almost ascetic reserve holds sway here. Space – indeed space given over to the Berlin climate – as an end in itself, as luxury.

The cool aesthetic of the plaza's monotonous walls of glass, stainless steel and aluminium band detailing declines to indulge in historic reminiscences, yet it also performs a lucid futuristic translation of the myth of Potsdamer Platz of the nineteen twenties into the logic of a modern media concern. Show, action, pleasure for the masses, commerce – come on in! The gigantic roof-tent hovering over the plaza, an illuminated beacon visible at night from afar, promises urbanity in its commercially concentrated form: the circus. Intentionally or not, in his use of the tent form Jahn demonstrates his reverence for Scha-

vergnügens, so am Picadilly Circus oder der Place Pigalle würde sie nicht gestellt werden. Anders das debis-Areal. Hier verheißt der von den ambitionierten Türmen von Kollhoff und Piano gerahmte Blick in die Tiefe der Alten Potsdamer Straße – gesäumt von mehr als ein halbes Jahrhundert alten Bäumen, den Charme der alten Stadt. Geschichte, Konvention, *genius loci*, hier ist sie, die echte Potsdamer Straße. Hier wird der zum Klischee geronnene Mythos als Bild und als Adresse beschworen. Natürlich ist der Kollhoff-Bau der Potsdamer Platz Nr. 1. Damit der eindrucksvolle, ebenso elegante wie markante backsteinverkleidete Dreiecksbau von Kollhoff diese begehrte Adresse erhalten konnte, mußte extra noch ein nicht benötigter Eingang an die Stirnseite zur Kreuzung verlegt werden. Adresse als Teilhabe am Mythos. Aber auch ein Eingeständnis: eigentlich ist der „Platz" für die reale Erschließung der debis-Stadt bedeutungslos.

Geschichte als Mythos, als Adresse, aber auch als Bild: der Architekt Kollhoff legt Wert auf die Ähnlichkeit seiner zwei Sockelgeschosse mit Berliner Bürobauten der späten Weimarer Republik. Die „Instant City" (Karl Schlögel) schafft sich ihre eigene fiktive Geschichte. Zusammen mit dem schräg gegenüber gelegenen *Haus Huth* stiftet das Kollhoff-Gebäude die Anmutung einer Kontinuität der historischen Stadt.

Mit vielfältigen Blickbeziehungen in ein kleinteiliges Straßennetz baut sich das Bild der Authentizität im Verlauf der Alten Potsdamer Straße weiter auf: Traditionelle Straßenpflasterung und die alten Bäume sind die Stützen dieser Suggestion. Das dichte Quartier bietet auf kleinstem Raum alle nur erdenklichen Raumbilder der alten Stadt. Diese an mittelalterliche Städte erinnernde Vielfalt hat mit dem historischen Ort nichts zu tun. So gab es etwa die Gassen (u. a. benannt nach den Gebrüdern Grimm, die in der von Piano beseitigten Linkstraße gewohnt hatten) hier, in den Gärten vor der barocken Akzisemauer, natürlich nie; Gassen gab es nur in der Altstadt von Berlin, die heute nicht mehr existiert.

roun's neighbouring buildings. The question of whether this is good architecture is not important – and wouldn't be posed of other European mass entertainment magnets such as Picadilly Circus or Place Pigalle, either.

The debis development tells another story. Here, framed by the ambitious towers of Kollhoff and Piano, the view down the Alte Potsdamer Strasse along the rows of half-century-old trees conjures up the charm of the old city. History, convention, *genius loci* – here it is, the authentic Potsdamer Strasse. Here the myth, congealed into cliché, is invoked as image and address. The Kollhoff building is, of course, Potsdamer Platz Number One. In order to secure this coveted address, the impressive triangular building, both elegant and striking in its dark brick cladding, had to be given a superfluous entrance at its 'prow' end at the plaza. Even as the number above it stakes a claim to the myth, the door itself points up the functional irrelevance of the plaza to the debis development.

History as myth, as address, but also as image; Kollhoff prizes the similarity of the two floors at the base of the tower to Berlin office buildings of the late Weimar Republic. The "Instant City" (Karl Schlögel) creates its own fictitious history. Together with the *Haus Huth* located diagonally across from it, the Kollhoff building engenders an apparent continuity with the historical city.

With a multiplicity of visual connections into the dense network of small streets, the image of historical authenticity continues to build along the length of the Alte Potsdamer Strasse. Traditional street paving and the old trees reinforce this impression. The dense quarter presents all conceivable spatial images of the old city in the smallest possible space. This variety, reminiscent of a medieval city, has nothing to do with the actual history of the place. The alleys (two of which are named for the Brothers Grimm, one-time residents of Linkstrasse, which Piano removed) never existed here, among the gardens out-

Boulevard, Straßen, Gassen, Höfe, eine Piazza, zum Verweilen einladende Wasserflächen. Piano versucht, Stadt als Gesamtkunstwerk zu komponieren, und ihm gelingt ein Stimmungsstädtebau auf einem irregulären, wenn auch nicht historischem Grundriß mit romantischen Anklängen. Manche Kritiker sprechen gar von Gemütlichkeit, eine aus Bamberg zugezogene Bewohnerin fühlt sich „wie in einer Kleinstadt" – wir nähern uns dem Geheimnis Pianos.

Stimmungsarchitektur, Konzessionen an Ornamentseligkeit und Klassizismusliebe, wie sie nicht nur in Berlin jetzt weitverbreitet sind, waren aber von dem konsequenten Modernisten Piano nicht zu erwarten. Die Architektursprache ist eher freundlich unterkühlt, reduziert.

Atmosphärische Wärme will Piano jedoch erzeugen und versucht dies mittels einer homogenen Farbgebung des Areals durch erdfarbene, beige bis orange schimmernde Terrakottaplatten. Viele Kritiker halten diese Wahl für unglücklich, Dieter Bartetzko beklagt in der *Frankfurter Allgemeinen Zeitung* etwa den „anämischen Ton" der Keramik in „kränkelndem Beige und Blaßorange". Durch diese bläßliche Grundierung fast aller, ohnehin etwas profilloser Gebäude nehmen die Straßen- und Platzränder, selbst die Foyers von Musicaltheater und Spielcasino die schemenhaften Konturen von Kulissenwänden an.

Als Hintergrund der in diesem Jahr erstmals am Marlene-Dietrich-Platz veranstalteten Internationalen Filmfestspiele konnten sich die Kulissen bereits bewähren, eine *location*, die, glaubt man der Presse, den Filmemachern gefällt.

Es könnte sein, daß sich diesen Virtuosen der virtuellen Welt der Charakter des Potsdamer, d.h. hier des Marlene-Dietrich-Platzes, als Ort gewordenes Filmskript erschließt. Die *virtual reality* zerstört nicht den Raum, sie erschafft ihn sich nach ihrem Drehbuch neu.

Damit offenbaren die städtebauliche Inszenierung, aber auch die Kulissenhaftigkeit der Architektur und die Miniaturisierung der Wolkenkratzer ein Leitbild, daß zwar die typischen Muster traditionellen Stadtraums zitiert, diese jedoch einem anderen Masterplan unterwirft:

side the baroque customs wall. Alleys were to be found only in the old town of Berlin, which no longer exist.

Boulevard, streets, alleys, courtyards, a piazza, inviting water features; Piano has attempted to compose urban space as a *gesamtkunstwerk*. He has succeeded in creating an atmospheric urban design on an irregular, if not historically founded street plan with Romantic overtones. Some critics have even spoken of *gemütlichkeit*, a word more typically used to describe the cosy, introverted comfort of a warm interior space. A resident transplanted from picturesque, Bavarian Bamberg felt as if she were "in a small town." We're getting on to Piano's secret. But sentimental architecture, concessions to ornamental fancy and the classicistic predilection currently widespread in Berlin weren't to be expected from Piano, the rigorous modernist. His architectural language is, rather, reduced and amiably cool.

Nonetheless, Piano wants to create atmospheric warmth, which he has tried to achieve by means of a common colour scheme for the development. The buildings are clad in terracotta tiles of earth tones ranging from beige to a luminescent orange. Many critics have responded unfavourably to the colour choices. Dieter Bartetzko, writing in the *Frankfurter Allgemeine Zeitung*, complained about the "anaemic cast" of the ceramic tiles' "sickly beige and pale orange." Due to the pale undertone of almost all the buildings, which are somewhat lacking in profile to begin with, the street- and plaza fronts, and even the foyers of the musical theatre and casino take on the flattened quality of stage sets.

These stage sets were put to the test this year as the backdrop to the Berlin International Film Festival, held for the first time at Marlene Dietrich Platz – a location that, according to the press, the filmmakers liked. It could be that the character of Potsdamer Platz – or, here, Marlene Dietrich Platz – naturally draws these virtuosos of the virtual world into its own film script-turned-place. Virtual reality

dem von Disneyland. Der Potsdamer Platz ist ein Themenpark, in dem wesentliche Motive von Großstadt in der fußläufigen, von Autos kaum gestörten Idylle einer Kleinstadt präsentiert werden. Die störenden Infrastrukturen von Großstädten, etwa der Anlieferverkehr, wurden in den Untergrund verbannt. Eine Prise Italien (Piazza à la Siena, Mailänder Büroblöcke), eine Prise New York, baugeschichtliche Zitate von den 30er bis zu den 70er Jahren, eine Prise Paris: der Boulevard mit seinen unzähligen Kaffeehaustischen – alles ist versammelt, nur genuin Berlinische Zitate fehlen. War Piano etwa der Meinung, ein preußischer Themenpark an der Friedrichstraße reiche?

Natürlich ist im Themenpark nichts wie im Original. So wurde etwa die Alte Potsdamer Straße optisch durch für Berlin untypisch hohe Blöcke verengt, gleichzeitig aber die Gehwege (für noch mehr Tische) verbreitert, die Fahrbahn verengt. Nicht nur ähnelt die Staße nicht mehr der alten Potsdamer, auch die großzügige Weite eines französischen Boulevards wird verfehlt, ebenso wie die dramatische Dichte einer amerikanischen *downtown*. Der Autoverkehr fließt auf der abgehängten Straße eher gemächlich, eigentlich ist die Straße eine Fußgängerzone: „Es herrscht eine wohltuend ungehetzte und angenehme Atmosphäre", so zutreffend die *Berliner Morgenpost*: Bad Berlin. Für richtige Flaneure – aber die gibt es ja nicht – ist sie zu kurz, für Touristen, die sich der endlosen Zumutung des Kurfürstendamms entziehen wollen (schweigen wir von Paris), ist sie genau richtig: Fünf Minuten hin, nein, zurück lohnt sich nicht, da biegt man doch lieber in die Passage. Schon wieder eine Prise Italien – Neapel, Mailand?

Die „Potsdamer Platz Arkaden", die etwas überraschend neben dem *Haus Huth* abbiegen, sind zwar keine Arkaden, also Rundbögen – eine Passage als vitaler innerstädtischer Verbindungsraum, wie er im 19. Jahrhundert Mode war, sind sie ebensowenig. Sie enden an der Eichhornstraße in der Monokultur von Bürohäusern, die das gesamte debis-Areal vom Landwehrkanal abhängen. Gerade hier wird

doesn't destroy space – it creates it anew in a screenplay of its own making.

Urban design as a production in a theatrical or cinematic sense, the set-like quality of the architecture, the miniaturisation of the skyscraper; together these aspects of the debis development reveal a model which quotes the typical pattern of traditional urban space, but subjects it to a different masterplan – that of Disneyland. Potsdamer Platz is a theme park in which significant big-city motifs are presented within the pedestrian-friendly, nearly automobile-free idyll of a small town. Irritating elements of the urban infrastructure, such as utility traffic, have been banished to the underground. A pinch of Italy (piazza à la Sienna, Milan office blocks), a dash of New York, quotations from the architectural history of the thirties to the seventies, a touch of Paris in the abbreviated boulevard with its countless cafe tables – all of this is gathered here. Only genuine ingredients of Berlin are missing. Did Piano think one Prussian theme park along Friedrichstrasse was enough?

Of course, nothing in a theme park is as in the original. Accordingly, the Alte Potsdamer Strasse has been optically narrowed by the atypically high blocks. At the same time, the sidewalks have been widened (to accommodate yet more tables) and the traffic lanes, in turn, narrowed. Not only does the street not resemble the old Potsdamer, it also falls short of the generous breadth of a French boulevard and the dramatic density of an American downtown. Cars roll easily down the oddly calm street, which is actually a pedestrian zone. "The atmosphere is agreeably unhurried and pleasant," remarked the *Berliner Morgenpost* as if describing a spa resort.

For true *flaneurs* – though there aren't any here – the street is too short. For tourists looking to escape the endless grind of the Kurfürstendamm, it's just right: five minutes there, no, the way back isn't worth it, better to turn into the "Arkaden". Another dash of Italy – Naples? Milan?

deutlich, daß eine Verbindung mit den umgebenden Stadtteilen nicht nur nicht gesucht, sondern bewußt verbaut wird. So dient die große Wasserfläche, die sich vom Marlene-Dietrich-Platz ausgehend bis zur Uferstraße am Landwehrkanal erstreckt, nur vordergründig den Besuchern als Ort zum Erholen. Als nur sehr flach mit Wasser überspülter Betondeckel (Reinigungskosten pro Jahr ca. 1 Million DM) schirmt sie die Einfahrt des großen Tiergartentunnels ab.

Nein, es führen nur wenige Wege aus dem debis-Areal heraus, indes führen alle Wege zu den Arkaden: Sie sind das ökonomische Rückgrat des Einzelhandels, mit über 120 Geschäften mittleren Niveaus auf ca. 35 000 m² Verkaufsfläche auf drei Etagen, unterirdisch ideal mit S- und Regionalbahn verbunden, sind sie zwar weder eine der größten noch eine der schönsten oder der reichhaltigsten, aber eine der erfolgreichsten Shopping Malls Berlins. Sollte hier das neue Herz Berlins schlagen, es fühlt amerikanisch. Deutlich wird dies auch an der mit Uniformen der New Yorker Polizei ausstaffierten privaten Sicherheitstruppe.

Diese Mall, von der Stadt ebenso wie vom Architekten noch einige Zeit nach dem Wettbewerb als amerikanischer Anschlag auf die abendländische Stadtkultur abgelehnt, wurde vom Bauherren letztlich erzwungen. Der zuständige Baudirektor, obwohl immer noch überzeugter Europäer, hat „inzwischen seinen Frieden" mit den Arkaden gemacht, die Mall stabilisiere den Statdtteil, der völlig „normal europäisch" sei.

Kritiker behaupten das Gegenteil: Das Quartier stabilisiere als „Urban Entertainment Center" die Mall. So fällt auf, daß in den Gassen, die nur als private Zugangswege zur Mall fungieren, aber auch in den Straßen und selbst auf der Potsdamer Straße nennenswerter Einzelhandel nicht vertreten ist. Die Mall hat das Monopol, europäischer Tradition entspricht dies nicht.

Damit erfüllt der Potsdamer Platz, identifizieren wir ihn mit debis, alle Kriterien einer amerikanischen Entertainment Mall. Hierfür spre-

The "Potsdamer Platz Arkaden", which obliquely and somewhat surprisingly open to the visitor next to the *Haus Huth*, are not truly arcades. There are no round arches to be seen, nor do they constitute a vital urban connecting space as was the fashion in the 19th century. They end at Eichhornstrasse amidst the monoculture of office buildings which set off the debis development from the Landwehrkanal. Here, in particular, it becomes clear that a connection to the surrounding districts is not simply neglected, but rather deliberately blocked. The large pond that stretches from Marlene Dietrich Platz to Uferstrasse at the Landwehrkanal offers calm and relaxation, though this is something of a pretext for its more basic purpose. The bottom of the shallow basin is also the concrete lid that masks the entrance to the Tiergarten tunnel off from the pedestrian area (at an annual cleaning expense of around one million D-marks).

No, there aren't many routes out of the debis development. In fact, virtually all paths lead to the Arkaden. They are the retail backbone of the quarter, comprising over 120 middle-range shops in about 35,000 square metres of sales floor on three levels, conveniently connected with underground, commuter and regional train lines running below the development. They are neither one of the largest nor the most beautiful or poshest of Berlin's shopping malls, but they're one of the most successful. If this is the city's new heart, it beats to an American rhythm, right down to the private security force decked out in what might be New York Police uniforms. This mall, rejected for some time after the design competition as an American attack against occidental urban culture, was eventually forced on both the city and the architect. The responsible building commissioner, while still a convinced European, has "in the meantime made peace" with the Arkaden. He describes them as a stabilising factor for the area, which is a completely "normal European" quarter.

chen die Konzentration von Musicaltheater, Spielbank, einem Multiplexkino mit den 19 erfolgreichsten Leinwänden Berlins (bei gleichzeitigem Kinosterben am Ku'damm), Disco, diverser Gastronomie und Hotels. Selbst die Wohnungen, von denen viele nur symbolisch genutzt, d.h. von Firmen für ihre pendelnden Mitarbeiter angemietet werden, passen in das Bild einer ganz normalen Stadt.

Natürlich gilt dies auch für Büros. Da Büros nach ihrer Adresse nachgefragt werden, lohnt sich am Potsdamer Platz – immerhin eine 1A-Lage – auch ein hoher Büroanteil. 80 % der Büros, zu einem Gutteil auch von den Bauherren genutzt, sollen vermietet sein. Hier rechnet sich Geschichte, denn noch hat niemand ein Copyright am Mythos des Potsdamer Platzes.

Mit dem „Potsdamer Platz" dürfte damit gelungen sein, wovon die Pariser oder Römer nur träumen: die Einrichtung eines innerstädtischen Reservats für Touristen, die so von der eigentlichen Stadt ferngehalten werden. Sollten die Berliner sich hierher begeben – nach einer Aussage der Arkadenbetreiber immerhin ein Drittel der Besucher – werden sie ebenfalls zu Touristen. „Am Potsdamer Platz darf sich der Berliner selbst als Tourist fühlen", so die bereits eingangs erwähnte Werbebeilage. Das Gegenteil der beschworenen Herztransplantation ist der Fall: Weder Herz noch Kunstherz der Hauptstadt, Mitte auch nur in einem geografischen Sinne, ist der Potsdamer Platz eine spezielle *location* für Stadtinszenierung. Derer gibt es viele in der polyzentralen Stadt Berlin: die Spandauer Vorstadt versucht zu sein, was Schwabing für München vor längerer Zeit war. Das Nikolaiviertel, eines der raren Produkte der DDR-Postmoderne, kommt in seiner Künstlichkeit dem Potsdamer Platz sehr nahe. Es bedient genuin kleinstädtische Gemütlichkeitsbedürfnisse. Die Friedrichstadt übt die Hochnäsigkeit der Hamburger Neustadt, der Pariser Platz hingegen gehört zu den Preußenthemenparks. Einzig die alten Zentren der geteilten Stadt zeigen die Gebrauchsspuren des Alters: Alexanderplatz und Breitscheidtplatz. Letzterem wur-

Critics maintain a converse view: the quarter as "urban entertainment centre" stabilises the mall. The visitor can hardly help noticing that in the alleys, which function exclusively as private access paths to the Arkaden, as well as in the streets and even in Potsdamer Strasse, there is a virtual absence of retail stores. The mall has a monopoly, which puts it directly at odds with European tradition. As identified with debis, Potsdamer Platz fulfils all the criteria of an American entertainment mall. The concentration of musical theatre, casino, a multiplex cinema with the nineteen most successful screens in Berlin (as the Kurfürstendamm cinemas successively close their doors), disco, and diverse restaurants and hotels testifies to this. Even the apartments, many of which are only symbolically used, i.e. leased by companies for their travelling employees, fit the picture of a completely normal city. This is also true of the offices. Since offices are sought by address, Potsdamer Platz, as a top location, warrants a high proportion of offices. Eighty percent of the office space here, in large part also used by the bank directors, has reportedly been leased. Here history pays off, as nobody yet has a copyright to the myth of Potsdamer Platz.

Potsdamer Platz would seem to have achieved what the Parisians and Romans can only dream about: an inner-urban reservation for tourists, so that they are kept away from the city itself. However, according to the operators of the Arkaden, one-third of the development's visitors are Berliners. "At Potsdamer Platz, even a Berliner can feel like a tourist," continues the newspaper advertisement cited at the beginning of this article. A heart transplant is the wrong metaphor for Berlin. Neither the heart nor artificial heart of the capital, and the centre only in a geographic sense, in reality Potsdamer Platz is a location for the production of urban images. There are many such places in this polycentric city. The Spandauer Vorstadt is trying to become what Schwabing was to Munich some time ago. The

den längst wesentliche Institutionen (Internationale Filmfestspiele, Berliner Festspiele) genommen, um die Bedeutung des Potsdamer Platzes als Standort zu puschen. Aber auch für diese Orte stehen die neuen kosmetischen oder chirurgischen Konzepte schon bereit.

Dennoch: das Experiment läuft weiter. Die Medien wollen ein Herz der Metropole, vielleicht schreiben sie es noch herbei. Vielleicht aber entdecken sie auch ihr Herz für die Wiedererrichtung des 1951 gesprengten Berliner Schlosses, denn: war dieses nicht das wirkliche Herz der Stadt? Somit eröffnen sich mit dem Mythos der Monarchie für einen weiteren Themenpark ungeahnte Möglichkeiten. Fragen wir Disney.

Nikolaiviertel, one of the rare products of GDR postmodernism, quite closely resembles Potsdamer Platz in its artificiality. It caters to a genuinely provincial desire for *gemütlichkeit*. The Friedrichstadt affects the snobbishness of the Hamburger Neustadt. Pariser Platz, in contrast, belongs to the Prussian theme parks. Only the former centres of the divided city, Alexanderplatz and Breitscheidtplatz, show the signs of use and age. The latter has long since lost significant resident institutions (International Film Festival, Berliner Festspiele) to the cause of promoting Potsdamer Platz as a cultural location. For them, too, however, the new cosmetic and surgical procedures are at the ready.

Nonetheless, the experiment continues. The media want a heart for the metropolis; maybe they will conjure it up with their pens. Or perhaps their hearts take up the cause of the reconstruction of the Berlin Palace, which was demolished in 1951. Was this not the true heart of city? The myth of the monarchy would open the door to unimagined possibilities for another theme park. Let's ask Disney.

Fassade der debis-Zentrale von Renzo Piano.

Facade of the debis headquarters by Renzo Piano.

debis-Zentrale, Blick in den Innenhof.

debis headquarters, view into the inner court.

Die Hauptzentrale der Berliner Volksbank von Arata Isozaki und Steffen Lehmann besteht aus vier unterschiedlich langen, paarweise angeordneten Gebäudezeilen, die mit Hilfe von dreistöckigen, brückenartigen Stegen verbunden sind. Zwischen den Baukörpern befindet sich ein gestalteter Stadtgarten, der vom Landwehrkanal aus einsehbar ist. Auffallend sind die Fenster und die Fassadenelemente aus braun-rosa Terrakotta – beide trapezförmig.

The headquarters of the Berliner Volksbank by Arata Isozaki and Steffen Lehmann comprises four horizontal building volumes of varying lengths, arranged in pairs and connected, bridge-like, by enclosed three-storey walks above ground level. A landscaped urban garden is located between the buildings and is visible from the Landwehrkanal. The facades are enlivened by alternating trapezoidal windows and cladding elements, the latter made of brown and pink terracotta.

Fassade der debis-Zentrale
von Renzo Piano.

Facade of the debis headquarters
by Renzo Piano.

Wasserfläche am Reichpietschufer.
Von links nach rechts: Staatsbibliothek, Musical-
Theater, IMAX-Kino, debis-Zentrale.

Water basin at Reichpietschufer.
From left to right: Staatsbibliothek, musical
theatre, IMAX cinema, debis headquarters.

debis-Zentrale an der
Eichhornstraße.

The debis headquarters at
Eichhornstrasse.

Am Wasser.

At the water.

Alte Potsdamer Straße:
Treppenaufgang.

Alte Potsdamer Strasse:
stairway.

Das Musical-Theater von
Renzo Piano nimmt die
auffällige Formensprache
von Hans Scharouns
Staatsbibliothek auf.

The musical theatre by
Renzo Piano echoes the
architectural language of
Hans Scharoun's Staats-
bibliothek.

Blick auf das Gesamtensemble mit dem Sony Forum, dem Sony-Hochhaus von Helmut Jahn und den Gebäuden von Hans Kollhoff und Renzo Piano, aufgenommen vom Dach der debis-Zentrale aus südlicher Richtung. Im Vordergrund die riesige grüne Kugel des IMAX-Kinos von Renzo Piano, dessen Rückseite in die überdachten Arkaden integriert ist.

The ensemble comprised by the Sony Forum and tower by Helmut Jahn and the buildings by Hans Kollhoff and Renzo Piano; view from the south from the roof of the debis headquarters. In the foreground, the giant green sphere of the IMAX cinema by Renzo Piano, the back of which is integrated in the covered Arkaden.

Eingang des Bürohauses von Richard Rogers. Das Gebäude ist achsensymmetrisch zum nördlich angrenzenden Gebäude und beeindruckt vor allem durch die extrovertierte Verwendung von Stahl und Glas.

Entrance of the office building by Richard Rogers. The block mirrors the neighbouring building to the north and is notable above all for its extroverted use of steel and glass.

Renzo Piano,
Fassadendetail mit farbigen
Sonnenmarkisen.

Renzo Piano, facade detail
with coloured awnings.

Der südlich gelegene Block des dreiteiligen
Ensembles von Richard Rogers ist ein reines
Wohnhaus. Obwohl es den Grundriß der beiden
Nachbargebäude aufgreift, weicht es in seiner
äußeren, komplexeren Form von ihnen ab.
Auch hier wurden zylinderförmige Elemente
in Wechselwirkung mit linearen Bauteilen
verwendet.

The south block of Richard Rogers' three-part
ensemble is purely a residential building.
Although it takes up the ground plan of both of
its neighbouring blocks, it diverges from them in
its more complex outer form. Here, too, cylindrical
elements alternate with rectilinear forms.

„Potsdamer Platz Arkaden".
Die dreistöckige glasüberdachte
Einkaufsstraße verbindet die
Alte Potsdamer Straße mit der
Eichhornstraße. Von der unteren
Etage gibt es einen direkten Zugang
zum Bahnhof Potsdamer Platz.

"Potsdamer Platz Arkaden".
The three-storey, glass-covered
shopping mall connects
Alte Potsdamer Strasse with
Eichhornstrasse. Potsdamer Platz
Station is directly accessible
from the lower floor.

In dem Gebäudekomplex von Lauber+Wöhr, dessen Hauptfassade zur Vox-Straße hin ausgerichtet ist, befindet sich neben dem Multiplexkino Cinemaxx das Hotel Madison. Die Stahlbetonkonstruktion ist mit Terrakottaplatten und großflächig mit Glas verkleidet.

This building complex designed by Lauber+Wöhr includes, alongside the Cinemaxx multiplex cinema, the Madison Hotel. The reinforced concrete structure is clad in terracotta tiles. Extensive glazing opens the main facade of the complex to Vox-Strasse.

Das Haus Huth als einzig komplett erhaltenes historisches Gebäude des Potsdamer Platzes wurde von Renzo Piano und Christoph Kohlbecker umgestaltet. Der fünfgeschossige Bau hebt sich mit seiner grauen Steinfassade stark von allen anderen Gebäuden des Potsdamer Platzes ab. Es dient als Bürogebäude und beherbergt neben einem Restaurant eine Weinhandlung.

The Haus Huth was the only fully intact historic building remaining at Potsdamer Platz. Its grey stone facade sets the five-storey building clearly apart from the rest of the buildings in the development. The interior, remodelled by Renzo Piano and Christoph Kohlbecker, houses office space and, on the ground floor, a restaurant and wine store.

71

Das Musical Theater und die Spielbank werden durch ein zweiteiliges Vordach miteinander verbunden, das von zwei Betonsäulen getragen wird. Zwischen beiden Gebäuden wurde ein ca. zwei Meter breiter Zwischenraum belassen, der von der Rudolf-von-Gneist-Gasse aus einen Ausblick auf die Staatsbibliothek gewährt. Eindrucksvoll ist die breitflächig verglaste Schaufassade des Theaters. Der Marlene-Dietrich-Platz, ein abschüssiger, flachtreppiger Vorplatz, verbindet Casino und Theater zu einer Gebäudeeinheit.

The musical theatre and the casino are connected by a two-part roof structure carried by a pair of concrete columns. A two-metre gap has been left between the buildings, allowing a view from the Rudolf-von-Gneist-Gasse through to the Staatsbibliothek. The wide, glazed facade of the theatre on Marlene-Dietrich-Platz is especially impressive. Marlene-Dietrich-Platz, a forecourt of broad, gently descending steps, brings the casino and the musical theatre together as a single architectural entity.

Das achtstöckige Gebäude des Hotels
Grand Hyatt von José Rafael Moneo,
dessen Fassade durch die gleichmäßige
Fensteranordnung klar gegliedert ist,
hat auf dem Dach ein verglastes
Schwimmbad.
Vom Hotel erreicht man eine Tief-
garage, die sich bis zur Varian-Frey-
Straße erstreckt.

Its regular fenestration lends clarity
to the facade of the Grand Hyatt Hotel
by Jose Rafael Moneo. The eight-
storey building features a glass-
enclosed rooftop swimming pool.
Beneath the hotel an underground
parking garage stretches to Varian-
Frey-Strasse.

Pool auf dem Dach des
Hotels Grand Hyatt, Berlin.

Swimming pool on the
rooftop of the Grand Hyatt
Hotel.

Blick in die Eichhornstraße
aus nördlicher Richtung,
rechts das Gebäude der
Spielbank.

View into Eichhornstrasse
from the north, right: the
casino.

Blick in die Alte Potsdamer Straße.
Im Vordergrund: Lichtschächte des Bahnhofs
Potsdamer Platz.

View into Alte Potsdamer Strasse.
In the foreground: light shafts of Potsdamer Platz
Station

Alte Potsdamer Straße.
Im Hintergrund Haus Huth.

Alte Potsdamer Strasse.
In the background,
the Haus Huth.

Das markante Büro- und Geschäftshaus von
Hans Kollhoff steht auf der Kreuzungsfläche von
Alter und neuer Potsdamer Straße. Die mit roten
und braunen Sichtziegeln verkleidete Fassade
erreicht eine Höhe von 101 Metern im nördlichen
Abschnitt und wird über die beiden Seitenflügel
in drei großen Absätzen abgestuft.
Ein begehbarer Laubengang in der 24. und
25. Etage ist für die Öffentlichkeit zugänglich.
Den Kern des Gebäudes bildet ein glasüberdachter
Innenhof.

The distinctive office and retail building by
Hans Kollhoff stands at the crossing of the old
and new Potsdamer Strasse. The facade of red
and brown brick rises to 101 metres in the north
section.
In the two side wings, it steps down in three
large sections to meet the height of the
neighbouring buildings. A pergola on the 24th
and 25th floors is accessible to the public. The
building is designed around a central court
roofed in glass.

Das sieben- bis neun-
geschossige Gebäude des
spanischen Architekten
José Rafael Moneo, das
vorwiegend Büroräume
beherbergt, im Erdgeschoß
aber auch gewerblich
genutzt wird, hat einen
trapezförmigen Grundriß.
Hinter seiner Stahl-Glas-
Fassade zur Potsdamer
Straße verbirgt sich ein
überdachter Innenhof.

The seven to nine-storey
office building by Spanish
architect José Rafael
Moneo contains retail space
on its ground floor. The
building is trapezoidal in
plan. The steel and glass
facade facing Potsdamer
Strasse conceals a covered
inner court.

Zusammen mit dem Kollhoff-Bau bildet das Bürogebäude von Renzo Piano und Christoph Kohlbecker, Berliner Sitz des Daimler-Chrysler-Konzerns, eine Eingangssituation zum neuen Potsdamer Platz. Die Kombination von unterschiedlichen Materialien wie Terrakotta und Glas läßt das Gebäude im Kontrast zur Backsteinfassade Kollhoffs besonders leicht erscheinen. Der spitze Winkel des fast dreieckigen Grundrisses wird betont durch das nach Nordosten weit auskragende Vordach im Erdgeschoß. Rechts im Bild das Jahn-Hochhaus von Sony.

Together with the Kollhoff building, Daimler-Chrysler's Berlin headquarters by Renzo Piano and Christoph Kohlbecker forms an 'entrance' to the new Potsdamer Platz. The combination of different materials such as terracotta and glass makes the building appear quite light in comparison with the brick facade of Kollhoff's tower. The sharp angle of the nearly triangular ground plan is emphasised by the northeast-projecting canopy at the ground floor. At right, the Sony high-rise by Helmut Jahn.

Das 24geschossige Bürogebäude von Murphy/Jahn schließt das Sony Center nach Nordosten hin ab. Seine gerundete Fassade und sein hoch moderner Glas-Stahl-Korpus stehen in deutlichem Kontrast zur schweren Backsteinfassade des benachbarten Hochhauses von Hans Kollhoff.

At its northeast corner, the Sony development culminates in the 24-storey tower by Murphy/Jahn. The highly modern steel and glass structure with its rounded facade stands in stark contrast to Hans Kollhoff's neighbouring brick-clad high-rise.

Deutschland-Zentrale von Sanofi-Synthelabo. Das neungeschossige Gebäude rahmt das Zentrum des Sony Centers im Bereich Entlastungsstraße/Potsdamer Straße, dahinter Filmmuseum und Mediathek. Dieser Teil des Sony Centers, der sich entlang der Potsdamer Straße erstreckt, besticht durch seine Monumentalität. Die Fassade wird lediglich durchbrochen durch eine mittig angeordnete Glasfront. Ein besonders auffällig gestaltetes Element ist die weit auskragende Eckstruktur im südlichen Gebäudeabschnitt, die die obersten vier Stockwerke umfaßt. Im Hintergrund der Sony-Turm.

German headquarters of Sanofi-Synthelabo. The nine-storey building frames the centre of the Sony complex on the Entlastungsstrasse/Potsdamer Strasse side. The Film Museum and Mediathek are located behind it. This part of the Sony Center, stretching along Potsdamer Strasse, makes its presence felt through an imposing monumentality. The stone-clad facade is broken by a centrally placed glass wall. The overhanging corner structure, taking in the upper four floors of the southern section of the building, commands particular attention. In the background, the Sony Tower.

Die neue Potsdamer Straße, die zwischen dem Sony-
und dem Daimler-Chrysler-Areal verläuft.

The new Potsdamer Strasse running between the
Sony and Daimler-Chrysler properties.

Sony Forum.

Sony Forum.

Im Sony Style Store.

Inside the Sony Style Store.

Sony Forum.

Sony Forum.

In der Bar im Urban Entertainment Center.
Die Beleuchtung der gläsernen Theke verändert
sich laufend.

Inside the bar in the Urban Entertainment Center.
The illumination of the glass bar continually
changes.

Blick auf die Dächer von
Sony Forum, Philharmonie
und Kammermusiksaal in
Richtung Westen.

View to the west, of the
roofs of the Sony Forum,
Philharmonie and Chamber
Music Hall.

Der denkmalgeschützte
Kaisersaal des ehemaligen
Grandhotel Esplanade mußte
aufgrund der Verbreiterung
der Potsdamer Straße
versetzt werden. Heute ist
er ein Teil des Sony Forums.

The Kaiser's Hall of the
former Grand Hotel
Esplanade, a protected
historic monument, had to
be moved due to the
widening of Potsdamer
Strasse. Today it is part of
the Sony Forum.

Sony Forum, Dachkonstruktion.

Sony Forum, roof structure.

Sony Forum, Dachkonstruktion.

Sony Forum, roof structure.

Blick vom Dach der Info Box auf das Sony-Areal.

View of the Sony development from the roof of the Info Box.

Sony Forum, Fassadendetail.

Sony Forum, facade detail.

Blick auf die Sony Europa Zentrale von
Nordosten.

View of the Sony European headquarters
from the northeast.

Bahnhof Potsdamer Platz, im Hintergrund der
Eingang zu den „Arkaden".

Potsdamer Platz Station, in the background,
the entrance to the "Arkaden".

Der Bahnhof Potsdamer Platz: eine unterirdische
Station für S-Bahn und Regionalverkehr.

Potsdamer Platz Station: an underground station
for metropolitan and regional train lines.